Adventures with a YORKSHIRE VET

The *Lucky Foal* and other *Animal Tales*

JULIAN NORTON

Illustrated by **Jo Weaver**

WALKER
BOOKS

First published 2023 by Walker Books Ltd
87 Vauxhall Walk, London SE11 5HJ

2 4 6 8 10 9 7 5 3 1

Text © 2023 Julian Norton
Illustrations © 2023 Johanna Weaver
Photo © 2023 Julian Norton

This book has been typeset in Miju Goudy

Printed and bound by CPI Group (UK) Ltd, Croydon, CR0 4YY

British Library Cataloguing in Publication Data:
a catalogue record for this book is available from the British Library

ISBN 978-1-5295-0992-2

www.walker.co.uk

MIX
Paper | Supporting
responsible forestry
FSC® C171272

CONTENTS

FOREWORD

AS WINTER DEFERS TO SPRING, vets and farmers get excited. There are changes in the hedgerows and fields: daffodils and primroses bring different shades of yellow, brightening the countryside. The brown mud in farmyards yields to bright green as new grass grows and buds burst into life.

In the warmer months, there is new life. Lambing time is in full swing and each day lambs arrive, then grow stronger and more playful, skipping and jumping in the sun. It's a hard time for farmers, though, with many long days of continuous work. For a vet, this is the hardest time of the year. Interrupted evenings and disturbed nights with little or no sleep are the norm, but this doesn't matter. Each newborn lamb or calf delivered in challenging circumstances removes any trace of exhaustion. It's a wonderful time and a pleasure to be out in the Yorkshire countryside, helping bring new lives into the world.

By summertime, some parts of the rural community are starting to relax. The annual show is the high point for most of the village and it's a chance to show off your favourite animals. In this, my second children's book, I've collected stories from the spring and summer – everything from lambs and baby alpacas to lumpy goats and sleepy tortoises. There is a mystery on one farm, with cattle behaving very oddly. And best of all (at least I think so) is a little foal who is very, very lucky. To find out why you'd better read on...

Julian

A Mystery at Willow Tree Farm

Once upon a time, an old farmer had planted daffodils in neat rows along the lane that led to Mr Dalton's farm. Today, they grew in abundant clumps rather than tidy lines, their glorious golden heads swaying and bobbing in the gentle spring breeze. As I slowed down to admire the drift of cheerful flowers, which signified winter was at last behind us, my faithful little Jack Russell terrier Emmy jumped up, pricked her ears and clambered into her favourite position on my lap.

She looked out, squeaking slightly in anticipation of a walk. I lowered the window so she could push her nose into the fresh springtime air, with just a hint of the nearby farmyard. It was one of my favourite smells too. Beyond the daffodils, in the distance I could see the herd, intently chewing on the lush spring grass. I guessed they'd just been turned out after the long winter months of housing. This was as happy a time for cattle as it was for humans and dogs.

But Emmy would have to wait for her walk because I had a veterinary mystery to solve. Something strange was going on at Willow Tree Farm. Mr Dalton was worried about his cattle and had called me earlier that morning. The receptionists were all busy so I picked it up and Mr Dalton was on the other end.

"I need a vet out to look at my 'eifers," Mr Dalton said gruffly, not realizing that I was the vet. "There's summat up wi' 'em."

"So, what exactly are they doing?" I asked, hoping for some clues to help me get to the bottom of the problem.

"Well, some of 'em seem to be confused," he explained, sounding puzzled. "They won't move around, and the ones that do move are wandering into things and banging their 'eads. Some of the others are behaving oddly too – one was walking backwards this morning."

Mr Dalton was clearly very concerned.
I checked the diary, where all visits and
operations were written down, and luckily
I could go right away. This sounded like
a challenge and I have always relished a
challenge. It was one of the reasons I became
a vet in the first place. That, and an unswerving
love of animals and a desire to help whenever
I could. I felt a thrill of excitement as I wrote
the visit in the diary and scribbled my
initials alongside.

**Mr Dalton, Willow Tree Farm – very worried,
cows behaving strangely, visit ASAP. JN**

I gathered what I thought I might need
and headed out, not sure of what I'd find when
I arrived at the farm. The dancing daffodils
made me smile as I drove down Mr Dalton's
lane, but I had the nagging feeling that I would

be faced with something difficult when I got to inspect his herd.

Willow Tree Farm was close to a river.
In fact, it was close to two rivers, as they joined forces less than half a mile upstream.
One came down from the distant hills to the north-west, the other from the moors to the north-east, and the nutrients they carried made the surrounding pastures rich and fertile.
Cattle had grazed the fields next to the farm for generations and had grown fit and strong.
But that was not on Mr Dalton's mind today as he stood, grim-faced, outside the cowshed.

"Thanks for coming so quickly. They're in 'ere," he said, stooping through a low door into a dark building, which was large but had a stuffy, dusty smell. There was a group of five cattle looking very sorry for themselves. Some were standing, staring at a wooden hay rack, which was precariously attached to one

of the stone walls. Another was gazing into
space. And a couple were lying down. One had
its head curled round, resting its nose against
its flank, as if fast asleep, and the other was flat
on its side with its eyes closed. I had to look
carefully to make sure it was still breathing.

"So, what happened then, Mr Dalton?"
I asked, trying to work out what on Earth
was going on.

"Well, the 'erd's been outside for a couple of weeks now," began Mr Dalton. "It's been dry and sunny, and the grass started growing early this year. It was lush and greener than usual, so I let 'em all out. It's been a long and 'ard winter, so they were as pleased to be outdoors as I was!

"Then, just yesterday, I noticed these few weren't quite right, standing still when the others were walking about. I hadn't a clue what was going on, so last night I brought 'em in, to keep an eye on 'em, like. And this morning, they looked worse. That's why I called you."

Some cases are simple to work out. But a group of older cattle with varied and unusual symptoms is a tricky thing to solve. Of course, and rather frustratingly for a vet, animals can't talk, so it's down to the vet to find the answers.

Mr Dalton had set the scene nicely and already I had a couple of clues with which to work. It was very useful to know that the problems had started outside, shortly after the cattle had been turned out, and that the rest of the herd seemed to be OK. I asked a few more questions, before reaching for my equipment and examination gloves.

"How long have you had them for?" I asked.

"I got 'em last autumn, from the sales. They were a feisty bunch, fresh off the hills in the Scottish Borders. They've been fed on turnips and 'ay all winter. And I wormed 'em and gave 'em all their vaccines after they arrived. They have grown well and looked in good shape. I thought they'd thrive on the grass this spring, but not so far!"

Despite the information Mr Dalton had given me, I was starting to get almost as confused as the cattle. Since they were showing different signs, I set about examining them one by one, starting with the two lying on the straw bedding.

First, I took their temperatures with my thermometer. Each one had a normal reading, which wasn't much help. A high temperature usually means there is an infection. A low temperature could signify a condition called milk fever, where the animal's calcium levels decline dangerously. But this is only seen in cows that have just had a calf.

Next, I reached for my trusty stethoscope, a vet's most important piece of equipment. It's made of two tubes with soft pieces that go into the vet's ears. The other end has a small disc that's placed against the animal, allowing us to hear noises inside their body. I love using my stethoscope because listening to these internal sounds gives me lots of information. Noise in the lungs can mean congestion or pneumonia. Listening to the heart tells me if it's beating at the right speed and with the right rhythm. Listening to the stomach or intestines lets me know if digestion is working properly. I set about listening intently to each of the heifers, but again there was nothing exciting to report.

I stood back, scratching my head. Next, I shone my torch into the eyes of each of the

patients, trying to tell if they could see. "Can
you see this bright light? How many fingers
am I holding up?" I wanted to ask. Certainly,
two of them didn't react to the torch, but it
was hard to tell whether or not they could
see. Maybe they just didn't have the energy
to react. Finally, I put on a long plastic glove
before feeling inside each of the animals.
This allows a vet to inspect important parts
of the stomach, checking for obstructions
or painful areas. I was being thorough, but I
suspected these investigations would be just
as unsuccessful as my other tests. I was right.

After half an hour, I was still totally baffled.

"What d'ya think?" asked Mr Dalton, as anxious now as he had been at the start. My rigorous tests hadn't eased any of his worries.

"I'm not sure," I said honestly. "There's no sign of any infection, but there's no sign of anything at all. Those two seem to have reduced vision." I pointed to the two heifers that were standing beside the hay rack. "But I can't put my finger on the cause, so I'll need to take some blood samples to send to the lab. I'm worried about some mineral and vitamin deficiencies, or it could be something called *Haemophilus* – it's an infection in the brain," I explained, trying to come up with at least some ideas.

"And 'ow much is this all gonna cost me?" asked Mr Dalton with concern. He was worried that these animals would die and there might be others that would become unwell too. Along with a big vet bill, I could see that his hopes of making a profit this farming year were evaporating in front of his eyes.

"I'm not sure – probably a few hundred pounds. Although I could just test the blood from one of them, rather than all five," I offered. "That would make it much cheaper." It highlighted another challenge faced by farm animal vets. Making a diagnosis could be hard enough, but without the opportunity to do the right tests, it was even harder. For many farmers, it wasn't easy to make ends meet. But we needed to know what was going on and the tests would help me diagnose the heifers and give me a chance of saving them from their mystery illness.

I gathered my blood sample tubes, each with different-coloured tops – green, red, grey and pink – and started drawing blood from the vein in the neck of one of the poorly heifers.

Then, I gave all the cattle injections of supplements and stimulants, guessing what might help them feel a bit better, and promised I'd report back as soon as the test results came in.

There was a sombre atmosphere as I washed my wellies and climbed into my car. I wasn't hopeful and neither was Mr Dalton. Emmy had been waiting patiently and she, at least, looked happy.

"Sorry, old girl. There's no time for a walk," I said as I scratched behind her ears. "I need to take these tubes to the lab urgently." Emmy was obviously disappointed that she wasn't getting a walk, but she was pleased to see me and wagged her tail regardless. Luckily, the laboratory was close to the veterinary practice, so I could drop off the samples on my way back, saving precious time. Every hour was critical.

The next day, Mr Dalton looked slightly more cheerful, but only just.

"Can we wander down to the fields to see the rest of the herd?" I asked as I climbed out of the car.

"They're down 'ere," he muttered. "Follow me."

I followed Mr Dalton through a gate and past a small clump of trees towards a sloping pasture next to the river. It looked like an idyllic spot – a perfect place for cattle to graze. There was a shallow muddy beach where they could drink directly from the river, so there was no need for a water trough in their field.

"A couple of weeks ago, this 'ole field was knee-deep in water," Mr Dalton explained. "We had some terrible floods and the 'erd couldn't drink from the river. The water can come up overnight if there's a deluge up in the Dales. It usually goes down within a few days, but it leaves mud and sludge everywhere. I don't mind, though, and neither do the cattle. All that muck is full of extra nutrients – that's why my grass is so good! There's been a farm near 'ere since Roman times. Look, that's where the original farm was, a few 'undred years ago, mind." He pointed to the ruins of a building on the far side of the river. He was obviously very proud of his land.

We turned our attention to the cattle. Most of them looked healthy, but there were two standing separate from the herd, still and subdued.

"Can you get those two inside?" I asked. "I'd like to have a look at them too."

"Aye, I'll do it later. I'll have to ask my neighbour to help me. If they do walk, they do it very slowly, so it'll take me a while. For now, come see what you think of the ones you saw yesterday."

The cattle inside the barn were still a sorry sight, looking distant and confused. They didn't seem to have made any improvement at all and I was disappointed my injections hadn't helped. I repeated my tests from before, listening to their breathing and shining lights into their eyes. I was now certain that some of them couldn't see properly. I wracked my brains for all the conditions that could make cattle go blind. Could they have vitamin A deficiency? It seemed unlikely. What about lead poisoning? Now, this was a possibility, especially since it can cause a range of symptoms, including cattle being subdued and stupefied.

"Is there any source of lead on the farm, Mr Dalton? Old paint, rusty car batteries?" I called out with renewed enthusiasm. Paint on old doors seemed to be a favourite for cattle to lick and swallow. And car batteries left rotting in the corner of a messy farmyard were another potential hazard.

"Nothing that I know of," Mr Dalton said, quickly adding, "but let's 'ave a look if you think it's a possibility."

"It would need to have been eaten recently, so it must be out in the field," I replied.

We hurried outside. I was hoping to find an old stable door covered in peeling, lead-rich paint that some greedy cattle had been licking. Maybe even one washed up by the river? After what seemed like an eternity, we'd scoured every inch of the pastures for anything that might contain the dangerous metal, but there was nothing. My latest and most plausible idea seemed to have been dashed.

"The thing is, Mr Dalton, there is a cure for lead poisoning, but we need to give it as soon as possible," I explained. "If there's any delay after a diagnosis has been reached, then the chances of survival get less by the day."

"And what about tests?" he asked hopefully. "'Ave we had anything back from the lab? Can we do any tests to check if it's what you think?"

"We've had no results yet," I replied, exasperated, "They might be with us tomorrow if we're lucky. But there's no test for lead poisoning. Well, there is but you need to do a post-mortem on a dead animal. So far, we don't have one of those."

"And let's 'ope we don't get any! You'd better start injecting these poorly ones first then if there's any 'ope of saving 'em."

This was the go-ahead to start some treatment. It was only based on a hunch. Without finding a source of lead the cattle might have eaten, it was a gamble, but one we were both willing to take. I started drawing up big syringes full of the antidote.

"They need this directly in their jugular veins and I'll need to repeat it tomorrow," I said. "And remember, there's no guarantee."

Mr Dalton held his heifers around the neck while I carefully lined up the huge dose of medicine that would counteract the poison – if indeed it was lead that was causing the illness. After each one, he'd pat the patient gently and say, "Good luck, girl" or "I 'ope you're feeling better tomorrow, lass."

The next day I was back with more

bottles of medicine and more hope. The two cows we'd seen in the field had been encouraged inside to join the others in what was becoming a hospital ward for cattle. Mr Dalton was with the animals and he looked and sounded positive. Some had been drinking water and had eaten hay.

I flashed my light into the eyes of each one in turn. Was there a glimmer of reaction?

"I think there's definitely some improvement," I said optimistically. "We should repeat the injections today and give a dose to these two." I pointed to the two new patients.

Later that day, results had come back negative for all the tests I'd asked for from the lab. My initial ideas had come to nothing, but the slight improvement after my treatment gave me confidence in my diagnosis of possible lead poisoning.

But where had the lead come from? It was still a mystery.

By my fourth visit to check on the poorly cattle, Mr Dalton was very cheerful.

"By Jove, you've hit the nail on the 'ead with your idea of lead poisoning, I'm sure of it!" he called as I arrived. "These cattle are almost like new today!"

Mr Dalton showed me the hospital pen, where every heifer looked almost normal. We both grinned widely.

After giving the heifers another round of injections, I headed off on my next call. Emmy was looking longingly at the passing countryside and I felt she deserved a walk. I'd been quicker than I planned at Willow Tree Farm, so I stopped by a bridge and we set off along the path beside the river, just upstream from Mr Dalton's farm. Em scurried in all directions, loving the chance to run around.

I stopped for a moment and admired the view of the river, imagining the stories it could tell. The flow originated high up in the Dales. As far back as Roman times, two thousand years ago, lead ore had been mined in that particular valley and used all over the Roman Empire to make pipes and baths. There are still mines there now.

Emmy was barking, desperate for me to carry on with her walk. She had pulled a large stick out of the undergrowth. It was dirty and covered in strands of duckweed, obviously washed up on the grassy banks from the recent floods that Mr Dalton had spoken about.

"Yuck, Em. Leave it alone," I called. "You don't know where it's been. It's probably come down the river from Swaledale!"

Then it struck me. Deposits of lead from higher up the river must have been washed onto the fields at Willow Tree Farm after the floods. That was the source of the lead that had poisoned his cattle! Not old paint or an abandoned car battery! I called Emmy and we sprinted back towards the farm.

"Mr Dalton, Mr Dalton!" I shouted. I could see the farmer among his cattle and frantically waved to get his attention as I ran down to meet him by the river.

"I think the lead must have come from floodwater on your fields." I gasped, doubling up to get my breath back. "In future, you must keep your cattle off the pastures after they've been flooded. The higher reaches of this river have deposits of minerals, including lead. It can be very toxic to cattle if the silt is washed out and deposited on the pastures.

I'm sure that's the problem. But with time, after the floods have subsided, the toxins will wash away and it'll be safe for the cattle to graze on the grass again."

A wide smile beamed from his face. "By 'eck, lad, I think you've finally solved the mystery at Willow Tree Farm!"

Double Trouble at Lambing Time

Janet was sitting in the middle of the barn when I arrived. The elderly farmer was perched on a folding chair – the sort you might take to the beach. Surrounded by bottles of medicine, sheep sprays and farming equipment, the deckchair looked out of place in a lambing shed. Janet had a young lamb on her lap drinking milk from a bottle with great enthusiasm. Its head bobbed backwards and forwards as the lamb guzzled the milk hungrily, spilling some down its chin and splashing Janet. Another lamb was walking round and round her feet, making high-pitched bleating noises and trying to get up onto her lap too, so it could get an extra drink.

Janet laughed. "Shoo, you've had your milk already! It's your sister's turn now, so don't be greedy!" The lamb didn't understand and watched with frustration as his sister sucked vigorously on the bottle. Janet was so engrossed in her task that she didn't notice me slip quietly into the barn. Most of the sheep had already lambed, but a handful of ewes were still waiting to give birth and I didn't want to disturb or upset them as they are easily frightened by new people.

Sheep usually have their lambs over a short period during the spring, which is nature's clever way of ensuring they arrive in time for the warm weather. The grass is green and nutritious, so the new mothers have plenty to eat and can produce lots of milk for the lambs to give them the best start in life. On this sunny afternoon in early May, one of the last ewes left to have her lambs was having trouble. Janet was an experienced shepherdess and didn't often need the help of a vet, but this year she'd had more than her fair share of tricky cases. So when she called the practice, I dropped everything I was doing, knowing it was a real emergency.

The farm was perched in a beautiful place, sheltered below the bright white cliffs on the edge of the North Yorkshire Moors. On a clear day, the views from the lambing shed stretched on for ever. It was a lovely place to be a sheep. And it wasn't a bad place to be a vet either!

Janet was passionate about her sheep and had developed a fine flock of stocky Suffolk

and Black Welsh Mountain ewes shortly after she retired when she and her husband moved to the North Yorkshire countryside. It had been her life's ambition to have a flock of sheep and she treated them all like friends. She consulted the vet whenever there was any cause for concern. Some farmers avoid calling a vet and try to carry out treatments themselves, but Janet wanted the best for every sheep, and I had come to know her very well over the years.

When she eventually caught sight of me today, Janet gently put the lamb back in the deep clean straw of a nearby pen along with her brother (who still seemed to be hungry).

The farmer looked tired as she slowly pulled herself to her feet. I knew she found lambing time hard work. Late nights, early mornings and many hours away from her warm bed, supervising the expectant mothers, meant that she was often to be found catching a few minutes' nap in that chair in the lambing shed with her sheep all around. As usual, she apologized for calling me out. "Thank you for coming, Julian. I'm so sorry to trouble you, but one of the last ewes is trying to lamb. You'll think I'm no good at all, but I've had a feel and I can't fathom what's going on. There are too many legs for me to work out! It'll be easy for you, I'm sure."

"It's OK, Janet," I reassured her cheerfully. "You know I love to help with lambing up here." I leaned against the lambing pen, watching the mums with their newborns. "But I thought you'd be finished by now though – there can't be many left to give birth. Has it been a good spring?"

"I've had a decent crop of lambs, Julian, and I have nearly finished. Just a couple more. But to tell you the truth," she confessed, "I'm jiggered. It's been hard work this year."

All vets – well, all vets that I know – love lambing sheep. The sense of joy and satisfaction in bringing new life into the world is a feeling that never disappears, no matter how many lambs you've delivered. And there are other reasons that vets like working with sheep. They don't bite and are usually well-behaved – unlike some cattle, which can aim a painful kick or charge around dangerously, damaging themselves and everyone and everything around them in their determination to avoid being caught. If sheep don't want to cooperate, it's possible to pick them up and move them around (but of course you can't do that with a cow). Sheep aren't too dirty either – sheep poo is neatly piled in small, firm pellets like chocolate chips, whereas cow poo is sloppy and splatters everywhere. I once saw a photo of a veterinary colleague who was standing behind a cow when it coughed. Liquid cow poo fired out at high speed and covered him from his head to his knees. Just two small white holes were left free of poo, where he'd managed to scrunch up his eyes in the face of the tidal wave! So, compared with cows and pigs, sheep aren't as smelly. Oh, and they're covered in warm, fluffy wool, which makes them nice to touch. Sheep can cause some minor inconveniences for a vet or farmer – they can be quite unreasonable, they never follow instructions and rarely use their brains – but on the whole, they're easy to work with.

"I've got you a bucket of water, antiseptic, soap and a towel," said Janet and picked up the bucket, shuffling along the straw-lined alleyway between the pens of sheep towards the patient. As we walked, she showed me some of her favourites. I nodded in approval.

"This is my last set of twins," she said, pointing proudly as we passed a tired-looking

ewe with two happy lambs. The lambs looked pleased with themselves, sitting on their mother's back as if she were a giant, fluffy cushion. From here they had a good view over the rest of the flock and I imagined them reporting on the action from the lambing shed. "Oh, that big new lamb has got stuck in the water bucket again! Silly thing…" "I wonder when we'll be allowed out into the fields to play?" "Mum's comfy, isn't she?"

"And this ewe had triplets. It's funny because she had triplets last year, too," Janet told me, snapping me out of my imaginings. "They're cute but a bit of a nuisance because they keep escaping. They're so tiny they can easily squeeze through the gaps."

In the next pen was Gertrude, who was patiently waiting for some help. I spent a moment watching her before climbing into the pen. It's a very good idea to pause, look and think before rushing in – a tip I'd picked up from wise and experienced vets when I was a student. You can learn a lot from observing animals before getting hands-on. Gertrude was lying on her side, straining every few seconds. She lifted her head and made a funny face as if she'd just smelt something unpleasant. I knew this was one of the things that sheep do when lambing is imminent. She shuffled, stood up, lay down and repeated the process all over again. There was no sign of any part of a lamb on its way out, so I knew it was time to get in and help.

We clambered over the wooden hurdles that formed the lambing pen where Gertrude was lying. I went first and Janet handed me the bucket of water and the towel, so she could use both hands to hold on. Once in, Janet wasted no time in getting a firm hold of the sheep around her woolly neck.

Gertrude offered no objection – she knew we were there to help. Before examining the distressed mother, I washed my hands in the warm water and then rubbed my hands and arms with lubricant.

The old ewe lay still and compliant in the straw as I made my first, tentative examination. Janet had already investigated before she called me and was concerned there were "too many legs". Of course, there is always exactly the right number of legs, but sometimes they are all in a jumble. With twins, there are eight legs in total – four per lamb. If more than two legs try to emerge at the same time, it can be very confusing to work out which legs belong to which lamb. Sure enough, just as Janet had described, there were lots of legs. I started counting and discovered there were four. Or at least four that I could touch. The next task was to work

out which were front legs and which could
be back legs. Was this two lambs, both trying
to get out at the same time? Was one coming
forwards and another backwards? Could it
be one lamb with front and back legs
all pointing outwards?

"What can you feel, Julian?" Janet asked,
eager to find out what was going on and if I
could offer any more clues.

"Well, I can feel four legs," I said. "And I'm
trying to slide my hand further in to see which

are joined to which body. I think they are all front legs so that means they must belong to twins. I can feel a body as well, but only one so far. And I can't find a head at the moment."

I like to explain what I'm feeling to a farmer, to give them an idea of how I'm getting on. Otherwise, without a camera on my fingertips, apart from trying to read the grimace or smile on my face, a farmer has no way of knowing whether I am making any progress at all.

"I'm trying to work out which legs belong to which lamb, but it's not easy," I went on. By now I was lying on the straw with my arm outstretched like Superman, inching my fingers further and further in around the tangle of lambs. Every so often, Gertrude would strain, trying to push out her lambs. And each time, Janet would reassure her in a comforting voice. "Don't worry, old girl.

Julian will soon have these lambs out."
She was more optimistic than I was.

"Right," I puffed. "I think I've worked
it out." It was surprisingly hard work. "I'm
going to push these two legs right back to
make more room for the other lamb." I took a
breath to adjust my grip. "Then I'll need
to find the head that belongs to these legs.
If that works, I'll be able to pull this first twin
out. The second should follow easily." By
now, it was my turn to be an optimist.

The second pair of legs seemed to be quite
easy to push back out of the way and, as
planned, this made extra space. I was right up
to my elbow and wiggled my fingers furiously
to try to make contact with the head that
belonged to the legs. I could just feel it, but
couldn't quite reach far enough to get a hold
and line it up.

"I c-can't quite ... manage to ... g-get the

… head," I stuttered between efforts and contractions, trying not to make too much of a big deal about how difficult it was. "It's there, Janet, but I just can't reach it," I explained. My fingers were starting to go numb, so I withdrew my arm and took a minute to stretch my hands.

"You're doing very well," said Janet, talking to Gertrude rather than me.

"Thank you," I replied, mistaking her comforting words as encouragement for me. "I'm frustrated that I can't reach the head. I'll get some more lubricant and have another go." I didn't want to rush her. My old boss used to tell me, "Plenty of time and plenty of lubrication" and it was good advice. If I couldn't reach the head, then the only option would be to carry out a caesarean section – an operation to cut out the lambs.

Gertrude sensed she could have a break

too and shuffled around, half trying to stand.
She was tired from the exertion and quickly
decided that getting up was a bad idea,
flopping back down onto the straw with a
thud. I got ready for another go – would I
be able to reach this time? Could I edge my
fingers just a little bit further?

Thankfully, Gertrude's shuffling had
moved things around a bit and the lamb's
head was now easier to grasp. "Good news,
Janet! I've got hold of the head. The lamb
must have moved into the space I made!
It should be simpler now."

But there was still a problem. The head
was bent down, so I could only feel the hard
curve of the skull, rather than the nose and
mouth. However, it was easy to sort out with
fresh fingers and renewed energy. I flicked
up the lamb's chin, lined the head up with
its legs, and moments later a slimy lamb was

lying on the straw. I rubbed its squashed face to encourage it to breathe but it didn't move. The next thing to do was hold it up by its back legs and gently swing it back and forth to free the nostrils and lungs of gloopy mucous. As I'd hoped, long, thick strands of slime cascaded from the newborn's nostrils, unclogging the airways. I lay the lamb down again and started rubbing it vigorously with a handful of straw. "Come on," I muttered under my breath. "Come on". Suddenly there was a gasp, followed by another, then a splutter and the lamb exploded into life, shaking its head and flapping its ears.

I cleaned my hand and arm before applying some more lubricant gel to deliver the other twin, which would be much more straightforward. Janet scooped up the newborn lamb and placed it in front of Gertrude, declaring, "It's a boy!"

Mum licked him all over, making small but rapid movements, only occasionally pausing for breath. Meanwhile, at the other end, I moved the second lamb into position so it could follow its brother out and into the world.

There's always a moment of anxiety when a lamb comes out. Will it be alive? If it's weak and not able to breathe, will I manage to revive it? But there was no cause for alarm and the second lamb started spluttering and squirming immediately. It wobbled to its feet and set off in search of a teat for a drink of milk, following its natural instincts.

Janet and I stood up, stepped back and admired the sight of a happy mum with two healthy lambs. It was probably one of the most challenging deliveries I'd done all season.

"Well done, Julian," said Janet.

"That was a tricky one for sure! Let's leave them to it for now. Come and see the older ones. They're out in the field next door. They'll look a picture in the sunshine today."

It was bright outside and we blinked as we emerged from the dark shed. The pasture was emerald green, with sheep and lambs dotted around like blobs of cotton wool. Young lambs have four main things to do – drink milk, nibble grass, rest or sleep (usually next to or on top of Mum) and play. On a warm spring day, playing becomes top of the to-do list and, as we watched, every type of lamb game was in progress. Groups of two or three were gambolling – running about, then jumping explosively in the air using all four feet. To show off, the more skilful lambs would add a twist or a flick, like a champion gymnast. There was a game of chase involving ten or more – they were going too fast to count –

running at high speed in large circles around the field. It was a joyful sight.

"I come out here every afternoon to watch them playing." Janet smiled. "They don't have a care in the world. Even when I've been

up all night, watching little lambs playing soon revives me!"

"And it won't be long before our twins are joining in those games," I said. "Then they can really put those legs into action!"

Toby the Sleepy Tortoise

In springtime, new life is appearing everywhere on the hills and in the fields of North Yorkshire. It's an exciting season, full of fun and new hope. But it's not just outside on the farms. Pet animals need help too, even some of the more unusual ones. Animals who don't usually live in Yorkshire...

"He hasn't eaten a thing since he came out of hibernation a few weeks ago," explained

Mavis, the new owner of Toby the tortoise. "And I don't know very much about him because I inherited him from my neighbour," she added. "Sadly he passed away in the winter. I'd promised him I would look after Toby, but Toby was asleep back then. I didn't get a chance to introduce myself to him until recently – when I inherited a cardboard box full of scrunched-up newspaper and a sleeping eighty-year-old tortoise!"

"We'd better have a look at him then," I said, peering into the box where Toby was sitting motionless along with a piece of cucumber, some carrots, half an apple, a slice of watermelon and a few green leaves. Not one of the tasty pieces of fruit and vegetables had even been nibbled. They were as untouched as Toby was immobile. He was quite a big tortoise, the same size and shape as a helmet that a child might wear when riding a bike. Like all tortoises, his shell was hard and brown with squarish patterns. Not much else was visible. His head and legs were pulled in under the shell, hidden from view.

I sympathized with Mavis. I'm not a tortoise expert – most of my patients are covered in hair, fluff or wool – but I've treated quite a few over the years and I enjoy looking after them. They are interesting creatures and always seem to have a story. So far, Toby was showing no sign at all that he had even emerged from his hibernation.

Hibernation is what some animals do in winter. It's like a state of deep sleep that allows them to survive through the coldest months. Hibernating animals use very little energy and can live on their reserves without needing to find any food to eat. Bears do this, as do bats, hedgehogs and bumblebees. Of all the pet animals that come to see a vet, tortoises are the only ones that hibernate over winter. Wild animals sense that winter is coming and find somewhere safe to hibernate – a pile of leaves (if you're a hedgehog) or a cave, deep in the woods (if you're a bear) – then simply go to sleep. Pet tortoises in Yorkshire rely on their owners to put them in a box and stow them safely in a cool place, like the garage or the loft. Some people keep a sleeping tortoise in the fridge. It may seem strange to put a living creature in the fridge, but it's ideal for a tortoise in November – so long as you don't mistake them for a crusty pie or a spare sandwich.

Under his sturdy armour, it was impossible to see if Toby was even breathing. I reached into the box to lift him onto the table. He weighed more than I expected but didn't wiggle or struggle as some animals do, so it was easy to get him out. I held him up and peered under his shell at where I thought his head should be. For a sleepy tortoise emerging from hibernation, this must have been peculiar. *I'm flying!* Toby must have thought, probably quickly followed by, *Or am I dreaming?*

When winter is over, and everything warms up, sleeping tortoises awaken, but getting them back to full liveliness can be difficult. I hoped and suspected this was the problem with Toby today.

"It's a bit like waking up a teenager very early on a Saturday morning," I explained to Mavis. "At first, they want to go back to bed. The body is still sleepy. Toby needs a boost, a bit like you or I would have a cup of coffee. Although you can't give a tortoise coffee!"

I put the tortoise carefully down on the table.

"But he's just not interested in anything

I offer to him," complained Mavis with worry in her voice. "I've checked on all the foods that tortoises like to eat and lined them up in front of him. The only thing I can't find is dandelions because they haven't started growing yet."

"I'll check him over first," I said, trying to sound reassuring. "There may be a reason why he won't eat. An injury or an infection in his mouth, for example."

The first thing I needed to do was weigh and measure Toby, using scales and a ruler. This confirmed that, although I'd thought he felt quite heavy, Toby was too light for his length. It wasn't altogether surprising, given his long months without food, but it meant that it was essential to get him eating and drinking as soon as possible. With difficulty, because Toby didn't want to be fiddled with and kept pulling his head back hard inside

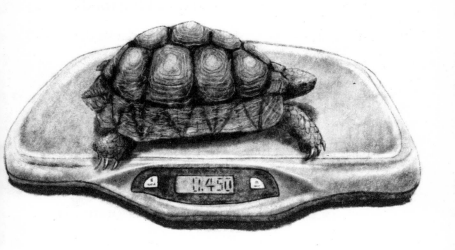

his shell, I opened his mouth to examine his tongue. Infections can be a reason that tortoises don't eat, but a quick check assured me that everything looked good.

"It's not easy examining a tortoise," I explained to Mavis. "But I think his mouth looks OK."

"And I suppose you can't tell what's going on under that shell," she said.

"No, you're right," I agreed. "It's not possible to do some of the usual checks I would do on cats and dogs, or cows and sheep. I just hope I don't have to do a blood sample – you can't imagine how difficult that can be!" I laughed.

In the absence of any serious or obvious diseases, I decided to give Toby a multivitamin injection to replace any deficiencies that might be holding him back after his deep sleep. I explained my plan to Mavis to try and put her at ease.

"This injection will help, and you should also bathe him twice a day in warm water," I suggested. "It will warm him up and help him rehydrate. Amazingly, tortoises can absorb water up their bottom, so it reduces the need for drinking." Mavis looked surprised but she agreed with my hydrotherapy idea.

"Let him sit in the sunshine too,
if possible," I went on. "Maybe an hour or
so in the greenhouse or on the lawn if it's
warm enough. And I should see Toby again
in a week when I'll top up his vitamins. If by
then he still won't eat, the next step will be
to syringe feed him with liquidized food. But
it's not a very nice thing to do and he won't
like it, so let's hope the injection works and
he wakes up!"

I waved the old lady and even older
tortoise goodbye. With my other hand,
I crossed my fingers. I was secretly worried.

A week later, Toby was back and the
waiting room was busy. There was an
emergency – a puppy had arrived with an
injured ear. He had got his head stuck in a
watering can and when his owner pulled
it out, the sharp rim had made a nasty cut,
which urgently needed some stitches.

"He's been putting his head in the watering can since he was very little," explained the pup's traumatized owner.

"It was fine when his head was small, but as he's got bigger it's been a much tighter fit. I'm not sure why he does it. Perhaps he likes the noise it makes when he barks inside it!"

Toby and Mavis had to wait while I sorted out the puppy. Eventually, I handed him back with a neat row of stitches.

"Come and see me in ten days for the stitches to be removed," I instructed. "And try to keep him away from watering cans!"

Finally, I called Mavis into my consulting room to check on Toby's progress. I quickly realized that my attempts to fix Toby had been much less successful than my treatment of the puppy's ear. Mavis shook her head, looking glum.

"He still hasn't eaten a thing. Nothing has passed his lips. He's slow and sluggish, and I'm very worried."

There was nothing for it. We would have to syringe him with liquid food every few hours. This would give him energy and get him moving, but he wasn't going to enjoy it much. I hoped that once he had some food in his stomach, he would start eating by himself again.

So Toby stayed at the practice for the day. The nurses mixed up some special powdered food with water and took turns to help with the feeding. Every two hours, the nutritious gloop was trickled carefully into Toby's reluctant mouth. It looked revolting and far less appetizing than the array of sliced fruit that had been lined up in front of him after bath time every day for the last week. By six o'clock, Toby was well and truly annoyed at the repeated indignity of having his head grabbed and his jaws opened for his regular doses of the liquid food. Whenever he saw a nurse or me approach with a loaded syringe, full of the browny-grey goo, his head swiftly disappeared deep inside his shell.

"I think he's had enough now," I said. "Let's leave him until tomorrow and check him again. Mavis can have him at home tonight and keep him warm."

The next day, Mavis arrived, still shaking her head and looking gloomy, although Toby appeared to have increased strength. His legs moved more quickly and his head bobbed in and out of his shell with more life. Was this the effects of yesterday's endeavour, already boosting his energy levels? Or did he just have a renewed determination to fight off the nasty vet squirting stuff down his throat?

"I'm not going to put up with that horrible experience again," Toby's face seemed to say.

But that morning, I'd had another idea that I hoped would wake up Toby. I needed to take Emmy for her walk and as we set off I took a detour. Emmy looked up at me confused. Morning walks followed a set pattern, through the fields and down to the river, pausing to look for kingfishers or chatting with other dog walkers. It was a peaceful time of the day that we both enjoyed. But today we turned right, rather than left, and into the cobbled market square. We were going to the local greengrocer's.

The sun was shining brightly and, even at eight o'clock, I could feel the beginnings of its warmth. I perused the delicious produce on display, which looked all the more appetizing in the sunlight.

"I'm looking for some tasty food for a hungry tortoise," I explained to the greengrocer.

"I don't need a lot, but it does need to be tempting."

I wasted no time filling a small bag with brightly coloured fruit and vegetables. I reasoned that if it looked tasty to me, it probably would to a sleepy tortoise too.

Soon, I had a collection of superfoods that

I felt sure Toby would not be able to resist.

"Let's go, Em," I said.

"Good luck," the greengrocer called after us cheerfully.

"I've brought in a picnic," I said to Mavis, explaining my earlier shopping trip. "Surely something in here will tempt him."

With a flourish, I revealed a plate of food fit for a king. Blueberries, mango slices, a strawberry, three bean sprouts, a small piece of banana, some spinach, peas, pieces of red, yellow and green pepper, and a radish. With Toby sitting stoically on the table, I offered him each food in turn. Compared with his response to yesterday's sloppy goo, the elderly tortoise was noticeably more excited – or as excited as a sleepy tortoise gets at least. Briefly, I felt optimistic. Toby sniffed the mango but didn't take a bite. The strawberry captivated his interest for a moment or two, but not to the point of tasting it. And he totally ignored the bean sprouts, even though I reckoned their crunchiness might have been appealing to a tortoise. Wrong again!

Feeling deflated, I primed the nurses to mix up more liquid food and prepare to hospitalize Toby again. Now the cold weather had passed and spring was here, Toby needed to start to eat of his own accord. Otherwise, he would die.

"We'll have to tube feed him again, I'm afraid, Mavis," I said despondently. Her face fell. She knew how serious Toby's condition was becoming and felt the heavy responsibility of looking after such an old creature. But she didn't like leaving him, as she had already formed a strong bond of friendship and trust with him. I promised to call her later with more updates. I'd give him a warm bath, another vitamin injection, more liquidized food and try to tempt him with the tasty fresh food morsels again.

The morning was busy in the practice, with other patients to treat as well as Toby. Fortunately, no other watering-can accidents needed my attention, but it was non-stop. I was happy when it was time to have a break for lunch. Outside the practice, we have a bench that catches the afternoon sun and is a fine place to sit and eat a sandwich, which is exactly what I decided to do. I'd earned it. But just before I tucked in, I remembered some of the earlier advice I'd given Mavis: "Let him sit in the sunshine, if possible." Of course! I rushed into the kennels to collect Toby to join me outside for lunch and picked up the bag of snacks.

Once back outside, I put Toby in the sun so he could soak up some warmth as I tucked into my sandwich. Toby's wise old head emerged on its wrinkled neck and strained round to peer at me.

"This is what you need to do, Toby," I said. "Just watch me. Open wide, food in, chew, and then swallow. If your blueberries, mango, peas and peppers are anything as lovely as this sandwich, then you will surely enjoy them!"

Of course, he couldn't understand anything I was saying, but I was trying to be friendly. I hoped my attempts would make up for the trauma of pushing the feeding tube into his mouth. After all, it's not often that I take my patients out for lunch! As I sat in the sunshine and ate, Toby studied me intently. Was he picking up tips? Even if he wasn't, at least he'd come out of his shell.

Once I'd finished my sandwich, I opened Toby's snack bag, chose a blueberry and put it in front of him. For a moment, he stretched his head towards the succulent berry, but then recoiled slowly. *If only he could smell the juice,* I thought. Toby might never have eaten a blueberry before. Maybe he didn't even know it was food at all! I grabbed a knife and cut the berry in half before repositioning it before him. The same thing happened – his wrinkly neck extended. I held my breath as Toby opened his eyes wide. Then, to my delight, he opened his mouth and grabbed the half blueberry. Slowly, his ancient jaws munched

and juice spilled down his chin. I cheered (but quietly so as not to put him off his food) and waved my arms in the air like a football player who has just scored a goal. Once the first half was gone, Toby made short work of the other half, chewing and swallowing more quickly and with renewed enthusiasm. I could hardly contain my excitement and shouted inside to the nurses. Soon, there was a small crowd of veterinary staff surrounding the tortoise and high-fiving one another as, one by one, pieces of food went down. Perhaps it was the warm sunshine or me enjoying my lunch that inspired him. Either way, Toby's appetite had reawakened.

A few weeks later, I'd been out on my rounds and had just finished treating a cow at Mr Dalton's farm. His cattle were back to full health after the problems earlier in the spring and he was his happy, optimistic self again.

Mavis lived near by so I decided to make a small diversion and call in to check on Toby.

"How's the old man getting on?" I asked when Mavis came to the door.

"Julian! How nice of you to drop by. Toby's doing very well indeed, thanks. He's in the garden. Come and have a look – if we can find him, that is."

But Toby was easy to find because he was in the middle of the lawn, greedily chewing at a dandelion.

"I see his appetite has come along nicely," I said, feeling a huge sense of relief. Once he'd finished the dandelion, Toby rushed off to the far corner of the garden, in search of another mouth-watering treat.

"He's so lively now, and such a star!" Mavis beamed. "I'm so glad he pulled through that terrible time after hibernation. He's become my best mate and such good company."

"He's done really well," I replied, laughing as he demolished another dandelion. "I'm delighted too. I still like to think that it was watching me eat my lunch on that sunny bench that reminded him what to do. They say an elephant never forgets, but maybe a tortoise does?"

A Foal Loose
in the Lane

The sun was already shining by the time
Emmy and I set out for her morning walk.
Emmy loved the summer, with its long days
for playing, and she charged off, bounding
through the top-heavy buttercups, which
were almost knee-high. Well, knee-high
to a human adult, that is, so they towered
over a small terrier. I expected she'd come

out yellow, covered in the flowers' brightly coloured pollen! Birds were chirping in the trees and hedges, and the sand martins dived into their burrows in the bank of the little stream, laden with tasty insects to feed their growing babies. Dragonflies hovered over the gently flowing water, their metallic blue and green colours shining brightly, reflecting the light. It was going to be another warm day. Emmy looked at me, wagging her tail hopefully, desperate for a swim.

"Not now, Em," I said, shaking my head. "Maybe later. We've got a busy day ahead." She glanced back at the water before skipping alongside me as we headed home for breakfast.

Work soon beckoned. A vet's job is always unpredictable, endlessly challenging and often full of surprises. The first thing to do when I arrived at the practice was inspect the diary. As the phone started to ring, more urgent and not-so-urgent calls were added to the list. Before long, reception received a call from a concerned farmer up at Apple Tree Farm, and the message in the diary read:

Foal loose in the lane.

I was intrigued as well as worried. Why was there a foal loose in the lane? Where was its mum? Had it been abandoned? Was it lost or injured? To answer these questions and help the foal, I needed to get on the road. I wrote down directions and headed for my car.

"Come on, Em!" I called. "We've got an unusual one first today. It's a baby foal!" She didn't need to be asked twice.

I hadn't been to Apple Tree Farm before and slowly drove along the twisting lane, looking left and right for the old stone buildings, which eventually appeared by a small cluster of oak trees. The farmers, Richard and Sophie, who had phoned the practice had recently moved to the area, so it was the first time I had met them. I pulled into the farmyard and parked near a likely looking stable. Even before I could get out of the car, the couple came rushing up and started talking excitedly, describing the events that had unfolded the previous evening.

"We were sitting outside, enjoying the last of the sunshine, when all of a sudden our daughter Lizzie spotted this little foal," said Sophie. "It was just walking along the lane."

"We couldn't believe our eyes," Richard added. "And Lizzie has already formed quite a bond with them. She's got a lift into town with a friend to try and get some powdered milk replacement from the farm supplies shop.

We thought that would be useful. The poor little mite probably hasn't had anything to drink."

Sophie continued her explanation. "We expected the foal's mother to appear, or at least a person who might be looking for them. But there was nothing – no horse and no owner. Just this little foal, walking along the lane all alone, as if it was a completely normal thing to be doing on a summer's evening. They seemed quite happy – not injured, worried or confused."

It was very fortunate that the lane was so quiet and there had been no traffic that evening.

"They were quite easy to catch," Richard went on, "which was lucky because we don't know much about horses and even less about foals! We just looped a rope around their neck and led them into that stable over there."

He pointed to a tumbledown stable with a rickety wooden door in one corner of the farmyard. "We thought that would be a safe place for them to stay overnight."

"Well, I'd better come and have a look," I said. "Em, you should stay here. You can watch from the car." I left the window open and Emmy sat on the passenger seat, peering out and cocking her ears in expectation.

Richard and Sophie showed me to the old stable. Judging from its appearance, the building hadn't been a home for any type of animal for many years. There were holes in the roof, the walls were partly collapsed and inside were mounds of mouldy bedding.

"Excuse the mess," said Richard. "We haven't been on the farm that long and we haven't got round to tidying the outbuildings. And we weren't expecting to have any animals just yet!"

I leant on the old wooden door, the top half of which was hooked open, and looked inside. A beautiful colt – the name for a male horse – gazed back at me, looking perfectly content. He had a narrow white stripe down his nose, a conker-coloured coat with black feet and tail. He was very handsome. I guessed he was just a few weeks old, no more.

"He's just a young one, isn't he? And there's no sign of his mum?" I asked.

"No. We've looked everywhere. It's just him," Sophie replied.

From a distance, the foal seemed healthy, but he was too young to be away from his mother. This was a mystery, but it was also a very serious situation. A foal, like any young animal, needs its mum to survive and thrive. It needs its mum for milk, for safety and to learn how to grow up and become an adult horse.

"I'd better examine him," I said and went back to the car boot, which was crammed with all my usual equipment.

I collected my stethoscope and thermometer. Importantly, I also grabbed the scanner for reading microchips. Like most animals, foals are supposed to have a microchip implanted under the skin on their neck by a vet soon after birth. The tiny chip, about the size of a grain of rice, has a number that is registered to the owners.

When a scanner is passed over the chip, there is a beep and the number appears on the screen, enabling a lost animal to be reunited with its owner. I've done this on countless occasions – sometimes with cats that have gone too far on their adventures or with dogs that have chased a squirrel into the woods and lost their way. Once, I even checked the chip of a tortoise. The elderly reptile had escaped from the owner's garden, shuffled under the fence and strolled off. Some days later, it was discovered emerging from under a pile of leaves in someone else's garden. The happy sound of a beep confirmed that he had both a chip and an owner. Today, I hoped I'd get that same beep as I moved my scanner over the foal's neck. But first I had to catch him.

Sophie and Richard had no head collar, so I improvised using my faithful but rather frayed and tatty rope halter. Normally, I'd use this for controlling head-strong calves, but it would work just as well for a foal.

"Steady there, little one," I comforted as I looped the old rope around the foal's ears and nose. He tossed his head a couple of times to display some objection to being restrained. But his protest was brief and I sensed I already had the youngster's trust. In the tumbledown stable, with such an old-fashioned way of holding onto the foal, I felt like James Herriot – a vet from the 1930s who wrote world-famous stories about his life working in

North Yorkshire. In Herriot's day, farms used horses to pull ploughs. Largely, those days have gone and fuel-guzzling tractors have taken over the role of a horse on a farm.

"He doesn't seem to mind the halter," I commented. "I wonder if he's used to wearing one?"

Sophie held the end of the rope and the foal remained calm. I checked for the all-important microchip, but sadly there was no noise from my scanner. Richard and Sophie looked at each other with disappointment. It would have been great if we could have reunited the lost foal with his rightful owner. Without a chip, finding who the foal belonged to would be almost impossible.

"Well, it looks like he'll be staying with us for now then – Lizzie will be delighted!" said Sophie, realizing the consequences immediately. Her daughter had already fallen in love with the colt and wanted him to stay. Now, this was a distinct possibility, but it wouldn't be simple.

"Rearing a young foal without a mother is hard," I cautioned. "There are lots of challenges and pitfalls. First, I need to check him over. If he's healthy, we can discuss the next steps."

I put my scanner back in the car, on the seat next to where Emmy was curled up, half asleep.

"This poor young foal has no owner, Em," I said. "I hope he's OK. I think he's found a new home, but this might be the start of many problems." Emmy tried her best to understand but didn't. She just yawned widely, then went back to sleep, tired after her early morning adventures in the meadow.

Back in the stable, I started my examination. The foal was remarkably relaxed and seemed quite comfortable around people. Some young foals don't like being handled and can get very anxious.

"Have you given him a name yet?" I asked hopefully. It's always easier to talk to a patient using a name.

"Well, Lizzie had a few ideas last night, but we haven't come up with one," Richard replied. "We expected he wouldn't be staying for long, but if we can't track down his owner, then I suppose we'll have to think of a name for him."

I moved my hand gently up and down the foal's supple but muscular neck. He tensed a little, just like when the head collar went on, but quickly relaxed again. I checked his mouth, and his teeth showed me that he was very young. Despite being lost and away from his mum, there was no sign of dehydration. His gums were pink and moist. His eyes were bright and wide, taking in his changing surroundings. I plugged my stethoscope into my ears and slid the end down to his chest to listen to his heart and lungs. Pneumonia is a serious risk in animals like this who have been outside for an unknown time, so I was anxious at first. But his chest was clear and his young heart was beating with a strong and regular rhythm. So far, so good.

Next, it was time for a temperature check and I carefully used my thermometer. The numbers on the display rose quickly up into the normal range, then slowed to a stop. The reading was bang-on normal.

I breathed a sigh of relief – there was no sign of infection. I felt his navel – the equivalent of a baby's tummy button. This is where the foal attaches to his mother before he is born. It can become swollen and sore in orphan youngsters, especially if they don't get enough milk in the first days of life. There was some swelling and it felt slightly squidgy, but the little foal was essentially in very good health.

I was about to explain my findings to Richard and Sophie when a car horn beeped as Lizzie's friend dropped her back home. Grinning with delight as she ran down the farm drive, she clutched a large pot of powdered milk specially made for feeding to a foal.

"Hello," she gasped, out of breath. "I managed to find this at the farm supplies shop. It sounds like just what we need. We mix it with water and let him drink it. The instructions are here, on the side."

When Lizzie realized that the vet had arrived, she suddenly became more serious and stared directly into my eyes. "Is he OK?"

"Yes, he's in remarkably good health, from what I can tell. I'll need to give him an injection to keep him safe from tetanus, which can be a nasty disease caused by bacteria entering a wound. Then the biggest challenge will be whether he learns how to drink. But, on the whole, this is a very lucky foal!"

"And Lizzie," added Sophie, "we're not sure if he has an owner, so we think he'll have to stay with us. At least for the time being." She winked at Richard, knowing that their daughter would be thrilled.

Lizzie's eyes lit up. "I can take care of him!" she cried.

"Rearing a foal like this can be very difficult," I explained. "He's going to need to learn to drink milk from a bottle rather than drinking natural milk from a mum," I explained. "If he doesn't learn how to do it, I'm afraid his chances aren't good."

Before I'd finished talking, Lizzie had run to the kitchen. Moments later, Lizzie reappeared carrying a large plastic jug with frothing foal milk sploshing over the sides.

"I've mixed it up according to the instructions," she said. "Now what do I do?"

"Well, first we need to try and persuade him to suck from a bottle with a rubber teat," I replied. "Have you got one?"

Sophie remembered there was a selection of dusty old rubber tubes and bottles in one of the outbuildings, which would have been used by the previous farmer to help newborn animals get the sustenance they needed. She scuttled off and quickly returned with a cobweb-covered plastic bottle complete with a rubber teat. It looked a bit worn but probably still functional. Lizzie poured some of her frothing milky liquid into the bottle, then carefully placed the jug in the corner of the stable, safely away from the action, so it wouldn't get knocked over and spilt.

What followed was a milky mess, because the foal did NOT like the idea of drinking milk from an old bottle with a stiff rubber teat. He spat and he struggled, and everyone ended up splattered with milk and saliva from the indignant young colt. He didn't want the teat in his mouth and he didn't want to suck!

"We'd better try another way," I suggested. "Or at least give him a rest. I don't think this is going to work."

Secretly, I was very worried the young foal wouldn't take the bottle. The simplest way to feed an orphan animal is to use a bottle with a teat. This method closely mimics how they would feed from their mum and is very successful with orphan lambs and calves. One thing was certain, the colt wouldn't survive without getting some milk, and quickly. I returned to my car to find a feeding tube. As I rummaged in the boot, Emmy woke up and sniffed the air, no doubt smelling the milk from inside the stable.

"Now where did I put my stomach tube?" I mumbled under my breath. "I'm sure it's in here somewhere."

When I eventually found it and returned to the stable, I couldn't believe my eyes. Emmy had jumped out of the car and found her way into the stable, where her whiskery face was deep inside the plastic jug, greedily lapping at the foal's milk. I was just about to shout out and tell her to stop but then I noticed the foal was standing with his head down, staring at Emmy. It gave me an idea. I gestured to Lizzie to lift the jug and offer some to the foal. Emmy might just have taught him how to lap rather than suck.

Having watched my little dog drink from the jug, the thirsty foal pushed his nose under the surface of the milk. At first, he blew bubbles and looked very surprised as white froth flew everywhere. The second time, he sucked and the level of milk in the jug slowly went down. I'd never seen a young foal drink like this before. He had watched my cheeky dog stealing a drink on a hot day and copied her.

"Now that looks like a good idea,"
I imagined the youngster had said to himself after watching Emmy. Within a few minutes,

the foal had drunk the whole jug, to the happy amazement of all the humans.

Even Emmy looked pleased with herself as she watched and wagged her tail, although she was slightly disappointed that there was no milk left for her!

"Well, what luck! It looks like this foal has learnt how to drink from Em!" I said. "Well done, Em, you've saved the day!"

"Mum," said Lizzie, "I've thought of a good name for our new foal. I think we should call him Lucky."

Lucky was the right name for him. Lost, then found within hours, he'd learnt how to drink milk from a jug in record time and, just as importantly, he now had a loving family to take care of him. I couldn't wait to follow the progress of this very lucky foal!

A few weeks later, at the end of another busy day, Emmy and I were passing the farm.

I pulled off the road and into a small lay-by near a bluebell wood and next to the stone wall that surrounded Lucky's field. In the distance, I could see Lucky. He looked bigger, stronger and more confident. His coat was already deeper brown, his tail and mane darker, and his socks brighter white. He was every bit as handsome and just as mischievous. His legs had grown and it seemed a long way down to reach the grass he was now nibbling. Even without a mum, Lucky was thriving in his new home.

"Em, I think this foal is a miracle." Em wagged her tail as usual, though I couldn't tell if she was happy about Lucky's progress, or if she was just excited about the prospect of a walk in the bluebell wood!

Olivia the Alpaca Learns to Walk

The first time I saw baby Olivia, she was slimy and surprised. I was just as surprised. I couldn't believe my eyes. Springtime for a vet is packed with births and new life. There had been many lambs, calves and the occasional litter of puppies. As spring slips into summer, the excitement for the arrival of fresh life on the farm changes, and we watch the youngsters grow and develop. But a new type of animal has appeared in North Yorkshire over recent years. I'm talking about alpacas and llamas, which have come all the way from the mountains in South America. Their thick, woolly fleeces are just as good at keeping them warm on the tops of Yorkshire hills as they are in their native Andes. These curious creatures are often born in the early part of summer, so they keep vets busy helping babies into the world after the thrill of lambing time has faded.

I had received an urgent call from Mr Hawthorne, a quiet and gentle farmer who owned a small herd of alpacas. He loved them dearly. "Can you come quickly? I've got a bit of an emergency. One of my expectant mothers is giving birth. She's in trouble and so is the baby." Mr Hawthorne was worried and spoke in a hurry, rushing to get his words out.

"Don't worry, Mr Hawthorne. I'm on my way," I replied, trying to sound calm and ease his concerns. Luckily, I'd just finished evening surgery and the waiting room was finally empty. It had been another busy day, but instead of flopping into a chair to make a few phone calls, and write up notes, I grabbed some equipment and headed for the door. "I have to go! I have an alpaca to see!" I shouted over my shoulder to my colleagues. They were used to this sort of thing because there are plenty of exciting dramas and emergencies in the life of a vet. Every day is different.

I wound my way along the narrow country roads towards Mr Hawthorne's farm as quickly as I could. These cases are proper emergencies, so there is no time to lose.

Alpacas, like horses and llamas, usually give birth themselves without difficulty. There is only ever one baby, so there's no chance that twins or triplets can be jumbled up. And because the babies (called cria) are usually fairly small, they don't tend to get wedged in the way a calf might. What they do have, however, is a very, very long neck and four very, very long legs. That makes five very, very long things and if they're not all lined up perfectly, they become a confusing mess. Imagine an Olympic swimmer diving headfirst into a pool. They are completely streamlined, with their arms held straight above their head. That's how cria need to come out of their mother, but their long limbs can get twisted together like a tangled ball of string. On this sunny evening, with a mother struggling to give birth, I knew that getting everything straight would be difficult.

The late-spring Yorkshire countryside was at its beautiful best. The hedges had fresh white blossoms from top to bottom and the grass was bright with life. The swallows had just returned from their winter holidays in Africa and flashes of red, white and blue swooped and dived to catch and devour juicy flying insects. They looked happy to be here. I felt as happy as the birds because I loved the countryside.

When I arrived at the farm, Mr Hawthorne was standing by the wooden gate with a bucket of water, shuffling from foot to foot with worry. He opened the gate wide as soon as I approached and waved me in with a dramatic sweep of his arm, spilling some of his water as he did so.

"She's over there, in that field," he said through the open window of my car and pointed into the distance.

This was both frustrating and exciting at the same time. I've spent many hours chasing animals around fields when they need help and the farmer hasn't been able to catch them. It's much better if the patient has been caught in a stable or small paddock before the vet arrives. Trying to corner a wayward patient can be tiresome and time-consuming. But, on the other hand, I do love to drive my vehicle across a field to do a job "al fresco".

Mr Hawthorne must have sensed my mild dismay and quickly added, "But it's OK. She's easy to catch."

Mr Hawthorne hopped into the passenger
seat and we drove slowly over the bumpy
field. The grass was short and the field was
dry, so there was no chance of getting stuck
in the mud, as can easily happen in winter.
I didn't want to spill any more water or
frighten the herd, so I inched the car slowly
and carefully over the ridges and furrows
of the pasture. Mr Hawthorne clung on to
the bucket on his lap with both hands. The
mother alpaca – like a pristine white ball of
cotton wool on legs – was standing still in the
distance, watching the sun get lower towards

the western horizon. I screwed my eyes up to get a better look as Mr Hawthorne filled me in on the details.

"It's a real problem," he said, his brow creasing. "I found her just before I called you. You know, when I was doing my evening check around. That's when I spotted it. The baby has its head sticking out."

This is as bad as it sounds and happens if both the long front legs of the unborn baby are folded backwards. Unlike the streamlined position of an Olympic swimmer, it was as if this baby was diving into a pool headfirst with its hands behind its back! It's impossible for a baby alpaca to be born this way, as it gets wedged at the shoulders and help is always needed.

I stopped the car in the middle of the field, as near as I could get to Mum without frightening her. Although she appeared to be gazing at the beautiful golden sunset, she must have been completely confused about what was happening. I didn't want to add to her worries by scaring her with a car in her field. We quietly got out, Mr Hawthorne spilling more of the water as he did so.

"She should be simple to grab," the farmer said hopefully. "She's used to me and she's had a baby before. She's called Mildred."

Holding out his hand for reassurance, he spoke gently to Mildred and soon had a hand on her head collar. I followed slowly and said hello to Mildred. Unlike dogs and cats, alpacas don't usually like their heads being touched or stroked, but they do like comforting words. I explained to both Mildred and Mr Hawthorne what I thought I'd need to do to help.

"The baby has its legs folded backwards, like this," I explained and bent both my wrists to demonstrate the problem. Mr Hawthorne nodded, understanding immediately. But Mildred didn't of course.

"I need to give her an injection to numb the whole area so it doesn't hurt, then I'm going to gently feel inside and try to reposition the legs so they're pointing outwards."

Again, Mr Hawthorne nodded. Mildred continued to look at the sunset as if preoccupied with the colours. She appeared to be enjoying the view too.

By now, the rest of the herd had realized something interesting was happening in their field. A car had arrived, which was unusual. A strange man, wearing wellies and waterproof trousers and holding a large plastic bottle of lubricant, had got out and was talking to their farmer. Both of the humans were looking at Mildred, who seemed to have something wrong with her rear end. They all stopped what they were doing and came over to investigate. Alpacas are extremely curious creatures and this was a great reason to have a break from nibbling grass and find out what was going on. They gathered round and watched, occasionally making high-pitched squeaking and peeping sounds – noises that inquisitive and confused alpacas make.

I felt like I should explain my plan to the audience too, but judging by the indifference Mildred had shown to my explanation, I didn't think it would help. So I collected everything I'd need and got to work. First, I washed my hands in the depleted bucket of water. There was just enough left. Next, I lubricated my hand and moved it gently inside to try and get the baby out. I knew I needed to manoeuvre the legs round and forwards to solve Mildred's problem.

It wasn't easy. There was very little space around the baby's neck. I edged my slippery hands carefully down one side until I could feel the bent leg, then reached as far as I could with my outstretched fingertips to flip its foot up and towards me. It was hard work and delicate, but after some moments, SUCCESS! The first leg was up, lying next to the neck and aligned correctly.

All the time, Mildred gazed into the distance, every so often turning her head to see what was happening. The herd continued to watch, as transfixed as alpacas can be. And Mr Hawthorne watched too, barely able to breathe. The final spectator was the unborn baby itself who watched me, rather disconcertingly, as if to check I was doing everything correctly!

The second leg was harder to reach and I grimaced and groaned. Finally, with some huffing and puffing, I managed to reach the second leg, flick up its foot and gently slot it into position. With the baby now all lined up, the next bit was simple and the cria slid out.

"Oh, thank goodness," exclaimed Mr Hawthorne, now grinning all over his face. "Well done, Julian. I was worried sick. Look! It's a girl!"

The onlookers were less impressed, realizing the alpaca had only been in the process of giving birth. There was no mass celebration from the crowd and they quickly lost interest. After all, there was grass to be eaten and they gradually dispersed to continue with this essential task.

"I'm going to call her Olivia," Mr Hawthorne said suddenly. "She's a beautiful little thing and that's a pretty name. It'll suit her perfectly."

Olivia soon wobbled to her feet and Mildred finally had a chance to meet her long-overdue baby, nuzzling and licking her gently. They were both tired, but natural mothering instincts are strong and a newborn has a yearning thirst for milk. We stood back and watched Olivia take her first sips of Mum's milk. As the orange sun slid further towards the horizon, Mr Hawthorne and I smiled. Nature is a wonderful thing. Just occasionally, though, it needs a helping hand.

It had been another successful day. Weary, I headed home, as the sun eventually dipped out of sight, for a well-earned tea.

It wasn't long before I met Olivia again. She'd thrived over her first few days, enjoying the life of a young alpaca in a small herd. But there was another problem. Both her front legs had developed a bend, with the feet pointing outwards.

This wasn't normal and Mr Hawthorne was once again concerned. I asked if he could bring Olivia to the practice so I could have a look. This was a slightly unusual thing to do because vets usually travel to visit farm animal patients on the farm. Alpacas, however – especially ones that are less than a week old – are easy to carry. Also, as Mr Hawthorne explained the problem on the phone, I suspected I'd need copious amounts of bandages. I kept only a small box of bandages in my car boot, but we had a generous supply at the practice.

So in the waiting room, at the end of afternoon surgery, there was a rather unusual and very cute creature sitting on her owner's lap, next to a cat in a basket and a very confused beagle, who had never seen a baby alpaca before. I took a moment to catch the expression on the dog's face. *What on Earth is that?* he must have been thinking. *That's the fluffiest dog I've ever seen. And her neck is SOOO long.* But the beagle didn't have long to stare, because I called Mr Hawthorne and Olivia in for an examination.

I was pleased to see that Olivia was thriving and standing on her own four feet – a far cry from the precarious position she had been in when we first met. However, it was immediately clear that I needed to apply stiff bandages to both her front legs. The joints were slack and loose and supporting them with bandages would keep them lined up, preventing further deformity. I gathered my equipment and started to apply layers of cotton wool, alternating with stretchy blue bandages, which would compress the cotton wool to make a sturdy splint. Before long, Olivia looked as if she were wearing some very snazzy blue boots, extending from her front feet to the top of her long legs. Her legs didn't bend in all directions as they had before, but poor Olivia tottered about like a circus performer on stilts. It looked as if it might take her some time to get used to her new boots. But to our amazement, within a few minutes, she'd got the hang of them and was strutting around the consulting room.

"I'm just going to go for a walk around the waiting room," Olivia seemed to say as she headed to the door and nuzzled it open. "Do you like my fancy new boots?" she said to a couple of chatting farmers. They did a double take when they saw the stiff-legged alpaca striding past like a model on a catwalk.

"Mr Hawthorne, I think Olivia is ready for you to take her home," I said. " Do you need a hand with getting her into the car?"

"Yes, please, Julian. But it looks like she wants to stay here in your surgery!" he replied.

I scooped Olivia up and placed her in the passenger seat, making sure I fastened the seat belt properly. I'd never put an alpaca in a car, but Olivia looked very comfortable and safe, even though all she wanted to do was try out her new boots!

I waved as Mr Hawthorne set off, with the young alpaca looking out of the window, heading back to the farm. For the second time in a week, I'd helped Olivia out of a predicament. For a moment, I thought I'd seen her wave a front hoof as if to say, "Thank you."

Two weeks later, Mr Hawthorne was on the phone again, wanting to know when I could remove the bandages. It's a fine balance – they need to stay on for long enough to allow the bendy joints to straighten, but not so long that muscles and tendons get weak from not being used. We also needed to make sure the skin underneath wasn't getting sore.

I arranged to visit back to the sunny field where we had first met. There were plenty of farms near to Mr Hawthorne and it was easy to find time to drop in when I was in the area. I wanted to see Olivia running around, pain-free and with straight legs, enjoying life as part of the herd, and I was looking forward to seeing her. I felt like a proud uncle as I returned to the alpaca field and I could see Olivia was growing well. Her long legs looked straight and the worrying angles had disappeared. As we watched Olivia trotting along, still in her blue boots, it occurred to me that we'd have to catch her. It wasn't so easy this time round and Mr Hawthorne and I were both sweating by the time we'd finally pinned her into a corner.

Olivia wasn't very pleased to see us and tried to escape, wriggling around awkwardly. Snipping off the blue bandages was fiddly but I was anxious to see whether the splints would need to go back on for another few weeks. Would the legs still be bent? Would they support the weight of her growing body? Now was the moment of truth.

Eventually, I managed to remove both bandages and was delighted to see two perfectly straight legs. I'm sure Olivia knew I'd been helping her, even though the bandages had been a clumsy inconvenience. As we prepared to let the youngster run back to her mother, I bent down to whisper some quiet words of advice in her woolly ear, "Be careful and don't run too fast. You'll have to get used to your legs feeling a bit funny." But she was off in a flash, running steady and strong across the luscious field. Olivia's once troublesome legs now worked perfectly and she danced freely. With a hop and a skip, and just before she rejoined the rest of the herd, Olivia turned her head towards us and made a high-pitched squeaking sound. I'm still not fluent in the alpaca language, but I like to think it was alpaca for "Thank you!"

Show Time!

The weekend of the annual agricultural show
was fast approaching. Everyone was excited.
It was a great day, with the best of North
Yorkshire's animals entered for competitions
to be in with a chance of winning a coveted
rosette, from cows, sheep, horses and dogs
all at their finest – not forgetting rabbits and
a handful of pigeons! There was even a tent
with cakes, loaves of bread, pots of jam and
vegetables on display. For the little village

of Stainforth, the show was one of the highlights of the summer. And over the last few weeks, I'd been watching as the grass in the show field was mown and tidied until it resembled a velvety green carpet.

This year, the dog competition was the focus of my attention. It was tradition for one of the vets from the local practice to do the judging. As I was the newest vet, I was quickly volunteered. The retired senior partner of the practice, Alistair, called in to see me during a gap in morning surgery. Everyone in the area knew him – his angular face, though worn and aged by years of working outside, wore a permanent smile. From my consulting room window, I watched him approach. Slightly stooped, he walked more briskly than his posture suggested was possible, but his progress was slowed by frequent stops to talk to people in the high street. He was a much-loved local character and always had plenty to talk about.

"Julian, we wondered if you'd like to judge the dog competition this year?" Alistair asked, once in my room. "I've been doing it for years and we all think it would be lovely to give you the chance. Handing over the baton, so to speak." Then with a broad smile, he added, "I suppose it's more like handing over the stethoscope!"

"Thank you, Alistair. That would be a great honour," I replied. "I'd be delighted. And will I actually need a stethoscope?"

"No, no. It's not like the kind of competition you see on TV. There are categories for 'waggiest tail', the 'dog with the cutest eyes' and the 'dog who looks most like its owner'. You know, that sort of thing. It's a wonderful afternoon and the whole village comes out to support it.

It's a lot of fun and nobody takes it very seriously." He grinned reassuringly.

It sounded simple and entertaining, but little did I know what pressure would rest on my shoulders when it came to judging the competition!

Later that day, the nurses were crowded around one of our newest patients at the practice, Bonny.

The fluffy puppy wagged her tail constantly and her tongue occasionally poked from her open mouth as if she were smiling. Bonny seemed unperturbed by the large pink swelling beside her eye. Even though Bonny was happy, her owner, Mary, accompanied by her anxious daughter called Kate, was distraught.

"She was absolutely fine yesterday!" Mary said, alarm in her voice. She's been a picture of health and a normal, happy little puppy since we got her earlier this summer. Then, just this morning, this suddenly appeared!"

She pointed to a pink blob, the same size and shape as a baked bean, that was bulging from the corner of Bonny's eye.

Bonny, who was now up on my table, wagged her tail so vigorously that her whole body wiggled from side to side, completely unaware of what all the fuss was about.

The unsightly bulge was instantly recognizable. "This is a prolapsed third eyelid gland – otherwise known as a cherry eye," I explained.

"Because it looks like a cherry?" asked Kate, who was still clinging to her beloved puppy.

"That's right," I replied. "It's a common condition, especially in young dogs. Unlike humans, dogs have three eyelids rather than two and sometimes the tear gland in the third eyelid becomes swollen and red." I scratched behind Bonny's ear and she looked up at me with another almost smile.

"What can you do? Can you fix it?" Kate went on, clearly worried.

"Yes, don't worry! It's a fiddly procedure but fairly straightforward," I explained. "Bonny needs an anaesthetic and an operation to reposition the gland and it'll have to be stitched in place so it stays where it should be. Then she'll be as good as new!"

"Will I still be able to enter her into the dog competition at the village show?" asked Kate.

"I should think so. There'll be plenty of time for her eye to heal in the next few weeks before the show," I replied, trying to offer reassurance.

"Thank you!" said Kate with a smile. "Did you hear that, Bonny? We can still enter the competition together when you're all better."

I arranged to operate on Bonny the following day. Kate and her mum whispered anxiously to one another as they left the waiting room, worried about the prospect of her operation tomorrow, but also about Bonny's chances in the dog show. Kate had set her heart on entering the competition to show off her new pup and she felt sure she had a chance of securing one of the coveted red rosettes, which would signify a first prize. But now, with an unsightly eye, would Bonny's chances be ruined?

The next morning, I met Bonny in the waiting room. I fussed her ears as I reassured Kate and her mum. Operating on a pup can be challenging, and when there's a worried owner at home and a child who cannot concentrate at school until they know everything is OK, the stakes are raised. However, I'd done this surgery many times before and it was usually very successful.

In theatre, once Bonny was under anaesthetic, I focused on the problem and concentrated hard on where to make my first incision. I planned to tuck the bulging gland back inside the fleshy pink part of the eye, from where it had popped out, and stitch it in place. It's a bit like pushing a sleeping bag back into its cover, then tying it up so the bag can't come out. This simple description makes it sound a whole lot easier than it is, but after a while, Bonny's third eyelid gland had been securely stitched back in place.

After the operation, there can sometimes be swelling, which makes the eye look less than perfect, and this was the case for Bonny. I explained this to Kate and her mum later that day. While I was very pleased with the outcome, I could tell Kate was disappointed.

"Don't worry. I'm very happy with the surgery. You'll need to put these drops into Bonny's eye four times a day. They'll take away the pinkness and swelling," I explained.

Sure enough, at Bonny's follow-up appointment one week later, the pup was looking good.

"I've been putting the drops in Bonny's eye like you said," Kate reported.

"She didn't like it at first, and wouldn't stay still, but I made sure every drop went in."

"And her eye looks very healthy," I replied with relief. "You've done a great job with the drops."

"Can I take her to the show?" she asked. "It's next weekend. Do you think she'll be ready?"

"Of course, that should be fine," I confirmed. I didn't let on that I was the judge of the dog show. I would have to be impartial. Even if Bonny looked perfect, could I give first prize to one of my patients?

The show was just a few days away now and excitement was mounting in the village. Puppies kept appearing at the surgery, requiring vaccines in time to be entered in the dog show. One morning, an elderly farmer called Mrs Brown arrived with her equally elderly dog, Oscar, for a check-up.

"I'm thinking of entering him in the competition at the weekend," she told me. "He's twenty-two, you know, so I thought the 'old dog' category. Do you think he'll have a good chance of winning? He's very fit for his age, isn't he? I don't imagine there'll be many dogs older than him, do you? I understand you are the chief judge!"

She winked and pushed a large bar of chocolate into my hand. "Something to keep you going when you're hungry, son," she added. *Was this a bribe?* I wondered.

This generosity continued for most of the week. Everyone seemed to be trying to boost their chances by gaining my favour.
I promised myself I would be fair and unbiased, and not swerved by friendships, successful surgery or large bars of chocolate.

On the day of the show, I arrived at Stainforth Hall early. I knew it would be busy and I didn't want to be late. Besides, there would be plenty of friends to catch up with. Once I'd parked my car, I headed to find the organiser, Mrs Ball.

Mrs Ball lived in Stainforth Hall, which was a huge stone building with sweeping lawns surrounded by paddocks. The show had been held on these grounds every year for as long as anyone could remember.

Mrs Ball marched towards me, conspicuous under a patterned silk headscarf with a heavy tweed skirt, despite the mild summer sun.

"Julian! We're delighted that you've agreed to be the judge at our dog competition today," she gushed with enthusiasm as she thrust out her hand for me to shake. "It's going to be held over here, on the main paddock in front of the house.

What do you think? Will this be suitable?"

"This looks lovely, Mrs Ball," I confirmed.

Mrs Ball especially loved dogs and so the dog competition had become an important tradition for the village.

"We always ask one of the vets to judge and everyone felt it was time for some new blood," Mrs Ball added, emphasizing the last two words. It reinforced the fact that this was my first time. I was anxious that there would be a lot of pressure and I didn't want to mess up by awarding the prizes unfairly. It was impossible to give every dog a rosette and I hoped there wouldn't be anyone left upset.

"The dog show starts at one o'clock sharp," she added, before striding off to do more organizing. I glanced at my watch. I had some spare time to wander around and enjoy the other parts of the show.

First, I headed to see the sheep. They were

gathered into small pens made of wooden gates, in lines of about eight. In each pen were two or three sheep, neatly clipped and groomed, with their farmers hovering nervously near by. Some sheep and handlers were standing in the main ring near by, about to be judged. Janet was there, looking on enviously, though without any of her animals.

"I like to come and look, but I've never brought my own to show," she explained. "I love them dearly but I don't think any of them would win prizes. I can never clip them neatly enough!"

The Peckitt brothers from Hagg Farm were lined up in the sheep ring, though. Both looked smart in shirts, ties and clean white coats. I recalled the last time I'd seen them, during a cold winter's evening when I'd delivered a lamb with some difficulty.

Later that evening, they had, in turn, delivered my car out of the hedge after I'd skidded on the ice. I had to admit, they looked more comfortable in their rough farm clothes that evening than their immaculate show outfits today.

As I walked around the other animal shows, I bumped into a couple of my other patients' owners. Mr Bellerby was there with Gus, the pup he rescued from the practice earlier in the year. He was watching the sheepdogs get ready for the trials.

"Are you entering with Gus?" I asked.

"No! 'E's a lovely dog but 'e's not a sheepdog. I'm teaching 'im and 'e's learning but not up to this standard."

"He's grown into a fine young dog, hasn't he?" I added.

"Aye, 'e 'as. When I got 'im, 'e was just a big ball of fluff. Look at 'im now! A proper grown-up!" We chatted about how Mr Bellerby and little Gus had found each other after his old collie had died.

Near the horse ring, Lizzie was waiting with Lucky, repeatedly brushing his mane. They were entered into the foal category, though Lucky would be the only foal there without a mum! I hoped the horse judges wouldn't be too strict!

"Hello, Lizzie. Lucky is doing very well, isn't he? He must have got the hang of drinking his milk!" I said, impressed by the shine of Lucky's healthy coat and strong legs.

"Oh yes! Now it's the grass that he can't stop munching! He's about two months old now, would you believe it?" Lizzie replied. "We never found his original owner, but I look after Lucky on our farm now so Mum and Dad don't have to worry too much." Lizzie looked very proud of her young foal.

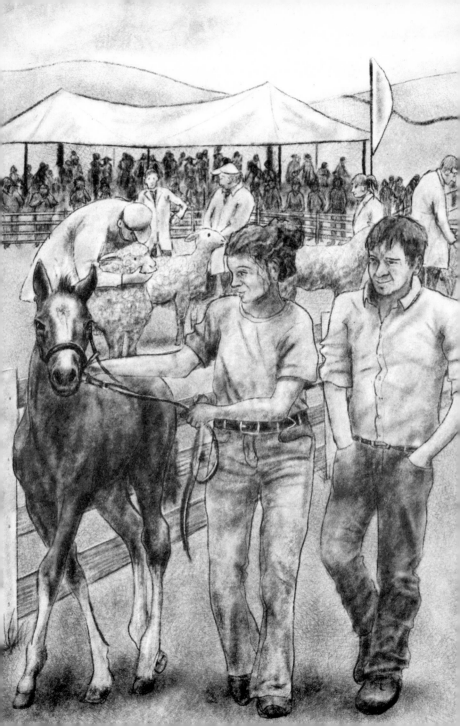

Joyce from Beech Tree Farm was there too. "Hello, Julian. I'm here as a spectator today! I've left Pigley at home asleep in the kitchen," she explained. I was relieved. Everywhere that Pigley went, calamities seemed to follow. A summer show was no place for an accident-prone pig.

"That's a good idea," I said. "Knowing Pigley, he'd probably want to enter the dog competition! Speaking of which, I'd better get going. I've got some judging to do!"

Under a small marquee, a table was piled high with different-coloured rosettes. Mrs Ball was next to it, clutching a clipboard with lots of lists.

"Ah, Julian. Just in time! We're ready to go," Mrs Ball said briskly. "This is your list of categories. Don't worry, I'll shout out each category, and then the dogs will enter the ring and stand in a line. Ask each owner questions about their dog and then look at each one in turn," she went on. "After that, you have to decide first, second and third. You tell me, then I get the rosettes and you give them to the winners. Don't be too slow, otherwise, we'll be here all day." She paused for a second, peering over her glasses. "But don't be too quick either, because we don't want any wrong decisions, do we?" she said slightly menacingly.

"I'll do my best, Mrs Ball," I replied, and took my place in the centre of the ring. I felt excited but also anxious. I didn't want to annoy Mrs Ball or – worse still – let Alistair down. All eyes – even the ones from the dogs – were on me. Glancing down the list, there were lots of categories, including "old dog" and "dog with the cutest eyes". I felt sure that Oscar would be entered, Mrs Brown hopeful that the bar of chocolate bribe would work.

Would Bonny be there with Kate? How could I make a fair judgement if she was?

"First category is the 'best male dog'," Mrs Ball shouted, and a stream of owners and dogs appeared. A line developed in front of me, and every one of the dogs wagged their tails appealingly. I walked down the line, following Mrs Ball's strict instructions. As each competitor walked around the ring in turn, beads of sweat developed on my forehead.

How could I choose a winner? They all looked wonderful. I began to see why the retired vet had been so keen to hand over the baton of responsibility! In the end, and conscious of the need not to be too slow in reaching my decision, I plumped for the miniature wired-haired dachshund for first place, a scruffy dog that lived at the dairy farm down the road for second. A schnauzer was third, mainly because he was wearing a smart red bow tie. It complemented his light charcoal-grey coat perfectly!

There was a gentle applause from the assembled and growing crowd. So far, so good. I ticked off the first round on my sheet. The categories progressed smoothly until the one for "old dog". Rickety, grey-haired old dogs tottered slowly into the ring. Oscar was there, Mrs Brown grinning widely and winking vigorously. I knew this category would be difficult, partly because it wasn't clear if I should award the top prize to the oldest dog (if so, surely I would need evidence of its age?). Or whether the winner should be the dog that was old, but didn't look or behave as old as it was?

After a brief examination and a chat with the owners – "She's eighteen, you know!" "He's not bad for twelve, is he?" or "You

wouldn't believe this one is twenty-two!"
from Mrs Brown – the old dogs wandered
around the ring at a much slower pace than
the previous entrants. It was time to stick
my neck out and make a judgement. I looked
at Oscar and at Mrs Brown, who I'm sure
was still winking at me, and at all the others.
Blocking out all thoughts of the huge bar of
chocolate, I stepped forward and handed the
red first prize to a fluffy Bedlington terrier
called Micky.

"Well done," I said. "He looks very good
for his age." The Bedlington looked grand
with the big red rosette on his collar, but Mrs
Brown stomped off, clearly upset. I heard her
muttering to Oscar, "That dog is nowhere
near as old as you, Oscar! That young vet
doesn't know a thing about dogs. I have a
good mind to lodge an official complaint.
They should get the old vet back next year!"

Next was another category that I expected would cause me a problem. "'Dog with the cutest eyes'!" shouted Mrs Ball.

More dogs appeared in the ring, all with very adorable eyes. I went along each one until finally, my eyes rested on those of a former patient. It was Bonny.

"She made it to the show!" said Kate. "And her eye is back to normal. Thank you, Julian. I'm sure you'll agree, she does have the cutest eyes of all!"

I stepped back for one final recap of each pair of pretty eyes staring up at me. Could I give the prize to one of my patients?

I took a deep breath and reached for the red rosette, trying to avoid the eager looks from the owners and the impatient gaze of Mrs Ball.

"And the winner is..." I paused for a moment, finally surveying the scene of dogs

with their appealing eyes. Bonny jumped up
and barked politely at me and the red rosette.
"... Bonny!"

A Small Goat with a Big Problem

All the animals on Ian's farm were mini. Admittedly, some started mini and then grew to be big, but most started small and stayed small. His small sheep were a breed called the Hebridean, which originally came from the rocky coasts of Scotland, where they would exist by nibbling seaweed rather than eating grass. They needed to be nimble and light to get down steep cliffs and quickly climb back up, to escape the incoming tide.

Ian had some tiny cows too – a variety
called the Dexter, originally from Ireland.
These cattle are about the same size as a
Shetland pony and have short legs. They
come up to a grown-up person's waist. They
were bred to make just enough milk for one
family, in the days when small farms kept
just a single cow per farm. Ian also had some
miniature ponies – who needed to be small,
once upon a time, when they helped pull

underground trains to move coal around
in mines – and a miniature Mediterranean
donkey – bred to grind stones for grain
inside houses.

Ian's collection of small animals,
whether they originated from the sunny
Mediterranean or the small islands of
Scotland or Ireland, had made a lovely home
in Yorkshire. But everyone's favourites on
the farm were the mini goats, or pygmy goats,

to give them their proper name. The word "pygmy" always makes me smile. The first time I heard it being used, I mistakenly thought the farmer said "pigsty". I couldn't understand why a goat would be called a pigsty goat. Did the goat live with a pig?

Pygmy goats are miniature version of normal-sized goats. They are mischievous, curious and full of adventure. They like to play and run, skip and jump. They also like to climb upwards onto the lower overhanging branches of a tree or – more easily – nearby benches and tables. Ian had arranged a sort of play area inside their paddock. There was a wooden structure with ledges and platforms. There was even a slide! On a busy day when I was visiting his farm to carry out the various jobs that need to be done by a vet, I'd always make time to stand and watch the little rascals taking turns to go down the slide.

The best and most popular way of sliding
was by standing on all four feet, adopting
a balanced stance like a skateboarder or a
surfer, and letting gravity do the rest. Small
hooves are quite slippery on a polished
wooden surface. Occasionally, some of the
mini goats would try sitting down, like a dog
or a child, but this way was slower and less
exciting. It was better on four hooves.

One of the goats was called Starburst. Starburst was even smaller than the others, and she had a problem. There was a lump on her face, on the side of her lower jaw. When Ian and the other goats first noticed the swelling, it was the size of a conker. At first, nobody on the farm was particularly concerned. But as the weeks passed, and as spring slipped into summer, the lump kept growing. By the time Ian called me to inspect it, the lump was about the same size as a small apple. Quite big for a small goat!

As we walked up the grassy bank to the paddock where the goats lived, Ian explained why he was worried. "This swelling on her face is getting bigger and bigger. I'm concerned it might be painful and I think it might burst. The other goats look at it as if they're very suspicious – I'm sure they must all be calling her Lumpy!"

I wonder what it is? I imagined they must be thinking, or maybe I hope I'm not standing near Lumpy when it pops!

All the goats stopped what they were doing when they saw me walking towards their field. I felt sure they must have recognized me as the vet. The man with the needle and syringe. The person with the cold stethoscope that listens to the noises from their insides. The one with the dreaded thermometer – they all knew where that went! I paused for a moment to look at the herd, watching them as they watched me, and looked for my patient.

"It's not me!" one of them bleated, in my imagination, before running to the back of the group. "You're probably looking for Lumpy," exclaimed another one. "She's the one with the lump on her face. Are you going to pop it? Can we watch?"

I was still in my goat daydream as Ian pointed to a tiny figure nibbling the lower leaves of a fruit tree.

"That's her over there."

Apart from the ugly swelling on her face, Starburst was a very pretty little goat. She had a small, smiling face, with bright and sparkling eyes. Her brown ears flopped appealingly and the little dangling toggles under her chin wobbled from side to side each time she pulled on the branch to get at another leaf. Starburst's coat was glossy in the sunshine, white with patches of brown. If it wasn't for the lump, she would have looked at the picture of health! I couldn't help noticing that she was alone, while the other goats were playing and chasing each other. Did she want to be alone? Was she happy chewing leaves by herself while the other goats played their goat games or did she really want to join in? Maybe the other goats wouldn't let her play, because they thought the pimple might pop in their general direction. Already I was feeling sorry for the little goat with the huge spot and I was determined to help.

However, spotting the spot was the easy part. It didn't seem to be affecting her ability to eat leaves or chew, but I would need to get a closer look.

"It'll be tricky to catch her," said Ian, matter-of-factly. "She's very lively and she's very good at jumping!" He laughed. "These pygmy goats go in all directions. They're very three-dimensional."

This would be our first and biggest challenge. Cows and sheep stay on the ground. They only go left or right or straight on, so you can round them up fairly easily into a pen or yard. But how on Earth were we going to catch a little goat that could go upwards as well and was currently free in a very large paddock with all sorts of obstacles?

Ian and I charged around, grasping hopelessly at Starburst as she dodged one way and then another. She most definitely didn't want to be caught and she certainly didn't want to be examined by the vet! The rest of the herd had scattered, hiding

under benches, behind rocks and in the faraway parts of the field, trying to look inconspicuous. They didn't want to be captured and examined either!

Eventually, we cornered the patient. Surely this was our chance to capture the rascal creature. But no! Starburst burst upwards, almost to the tree branches and nimbly escaped through our grasping arms.

Ian and I lay on the dusty ground, laughing at each other and our pathetic attempts to catch a small goat.

"It shouldn't be this difficult!" I said to Ian once I'd gathered my breath.

Meanwhile, standing on a large rock and munching another leaf from a different tree, Starburst appeared to be laughing too. She was laughing at us!

Eventually, we did manage to catch the rapscallion. In the end, two-legged and able-thinking humans should always be able to outwit a mini goat – even if that goat does live in a large paddock, and has the advantage of four legs and being able to jump in all sorts of directions.

Finally, I could get a proper look at the lump and make a plan. Being a vet is like being a detective. We have to look for clues to work out what's going on, then we can

decide what to do about the problem.
Of course, animals can't talk so they can't
say things like, "I've got a terrible headache,"
or "I'm lame because my toe hurts." Vets
need to ask the farmer or owner questions to
gather clues and then examine the patient,
put all the information together and make a
diagnosis. Already I had discovered that the
lump had been there for a couple of months
but now it was quickly getting bigger – the
other day it was just the size of a conker and
now it was a small apple.

Next, I started my examination.
The apple-sized swelling felt soft – there was
a slight squidge when I squeezed it. It was
near the lower jaw, which made it prominent.
It wasn't particularly painful and it was not
attached to deeper tissues. I felt fairly sure
that this lump was an abscess. An abscess is
a large spot, full of horrible pus that is often

very smelly. It must have been caused by a small scratch or a thorn from a spiky bush or tree. Maybe Starburst had been chewing on a branch and got a splinter in the skin over her jaw? I explained my thoughts to Ian.

"That's certainly possible," he confirmed. "She's always eating leaves and, as you've just seen, she loves to jump around at high speed. She's prone to accidents! What can you do to help?"

There were three options:

1) Leave the lump alone and hope it would disappear eventually. I suspected this wouldn't work.

2) Inject Starburst with antibiotics. This was a simple tactic, although Ian would need to catch her every day for a while to give her an injection. The antibiotics would counteract any infection, but I knew this wouldn't guarantee a cure.

3) Lance the abscess with a scalpel. Any pus would squirt out of the lump and onto the floor. It would immediately cure the problem, although there would be a small risk of bleeding or other complications.

I decided to go with option number three. During my time as a vet, I had lanced plenty of abscesses like this on various animals – cats, dogs, cows and sheep, and even the occasional rabbit. It was often effective and usually dramatic. I explained my plan to Ian and got my things ready.

I prepared an area at the most squidgy point of the lump by clipping off some hair with scissors and then scrubbing the skin with cotton wool that had been soaked in antiseptic.

Next, I reached into my box of equipment and found a small scalpel. My plan involved making a quick incision at the point of maximum pressure. Because the skin was stretched and the scalpel was sharp, it wouldn't hurt Starburst at all. I hoped Ian could hold her still for the minor operation because it was essential that she didn't move, let alone escape and run away. I readied myself to make the incision.

By now, the rest of the herd had drifted over to see what was happening. I felt certain they must have been waiting for this moment ever since they'd first noticed the swelling. Momentarily, I drifted back into my daydream, imagining their goat thoughts. *He's going to pop it! Will it be full of pus? How far will it squirt?*

"I've got her still now, Julian. I'm ready when you are," Ian said, bringing me back to reality.

"Yes, I'm ready," I assured him. "Don't worry, it won't hurt her. She'll just feel a scratch. Then, hopefully, the pus will drain out."

I took a deep breath and pushed firmly
with the scalpel. Its sharp blade made a
neat hole through the skin and into the soft
insides of the swelling. Starburst didn't react.
She didn't feel a thing. I placed the blade in
a safe place and, with two fingers placed on
either side of the lump, started to squeeze.
What happened next was quite incredible
and neither Ian, nor I, nor Starburst, nor any

of the herd of assembled little goats could believe our eyes.

A stream of thick, creamy pus poured out from my incision and cascaded like a fountain in a slow-moving arc towards the other goats. The jet of goo just missed Ian's wellies and my arm and hit the ground about two metres away from us. Starburst's eyes widened immediately with the relief of the released pressure. And the eyes of the onlooking goats widened even more, amazed at the spectacle. Three goats near the front of the gang let out dramatic noises and ran sideways for fear of being covered in gunge.

It was a few moments later that the smell came in a stinking wave that caused Ian and me to screw up our faces and exclaim loudly. "Ugh!" we both cried in unison.

I kept squeezing until the volcano of pus stopped flowing. The stream of sticky, smelly mess that lay on the nearby grass was impressive. Once the other goats realized it was safe, they came to investigate, sniffing and then recoiling one at a time. The smell was disgusting. Starburst, meanwhile, wondered what the fuss was all about, although it was clear she looked an awful lot better. The lump had gone and her face had returned to its normal shape and symmetry.

"Well, that was spectacular!" Ian said. "I've never seen that much pus in a goat before!"

"She should feel better now that's gone," I added. Inwardly, I hoped the other goats would want to play with her again and that she could rejoin their goat games. We'd know the answer soon enough. I gave Starburst a couple of injections – some antibiotics to counteract any remaining infection and a painkiller, to treat any soreness from the minor scalpel surgery.

"You can let her go now, Ian. I think I've done everything I can," I told the farmer as I started to gather my equipment.

Starburst skipped away, very pleased to be back on her own feet and not in the strong grip of a human. I stood back to watch the reaction of the rest of the mini goats, who came forwards one by one, sniffing Starburst and making little bleating noises. "Starburst! That was SO gross but SO cool!" "Come and play. We've got a great game planned for this afternoon." I was back in my daydream again but it seemed that Starburst and her friends had been impressed by the show I'd put on for them today.

Gilbert the Greedy Pig

The first time I met Gilbert he was a nuisance. I was in the field where he lived with his friend, Howard. The dray horse was an enormous Clydesdale horse – a breed originally used for pulling large carts and heavy work – and Howard was my patient on that sunny morning. Clydesdales are the biggest horses in the world, huge but gentle. Howard, it turned out, also had the biggest feet I had ever seen. I have never treated an elephant, nor come up close to an elephant's foot, but I imagined that the feet of Howard the horse might be even bigger than that.

It was a pleasant and tranquil scene, only slightly marred by my concern over how I would manage to examine Howard, whom I could see in the distance. With some trepidation, I drove my car towards a collection of tumbledown stables, crossing a bumpy field with mud baked hard by the sun. The rest of the field had tall grass, swaying in the warm breeze, the seed heads of each grass stalk hanging downwards as if weary from the heat. And there were drifts of buttercups like shining yellow jewels. Emmy, by now sitting on my lap with her nose out of the window, sniffed the sweet summer air, sensing the insects that buzzed by. As I drew closer, I could see Abigail, the animals' owner, standing with Howard, stroking his thick neck, offering reassurance for what was to come.

"Hello, Abigail," I said through my open car window. "Is it OK to park here?"

"Hello, Julian. Thank you for coming. Who's this? What a lovely little dog!" Abigail called, coming over to fuss Emmy's ears as she peeped her head out of the window, her bottom still plonked firmly on my lap.

"This is Emmy. She loves coming with me on visits, especially on a day like today," I replied by way of introduction.

"And this is Howard," Abigail explained, throwing out her arm with a flourish towards the horse, who was looking very miserable with his sore foot. "And somewhere in this long grass is my best friend, Gilbert," she added. "Come and say hello, Gilbert. There's a nice man who has come to help Howard. I'm sure you'd like to meet him."

I got out of my car and opened the boot to start gathering the equipment I would need to examine Howard's foot.

"You'd better stay here, Em," I said, leaving her inside to observe the goings-on from a safe vantage point. "You can watch from the passenger seat."

I didn't want Emmy to bark and risk frightening Howard, who might not be familiar with little Jack Russell terriers. And I didn't want Emmy to be frightened of whatever would eventually come running out of the thick grass.

"Come on, Gilbert. I know you're not shy. I have some of your favourite biscuits," Abigail called, rustling a packet. Within moments, Gilbert emerged. He was another huge animal, with a long and wide body, stocky legs and a deep, guttural grunt. Gilbert was a pink pig, though most of his body

was covered in dried mud, which gave him
a brownish-grey tinge. He had tiny eyes,
pushed close together and squashed by a
short, fat snout that was covered in the dusty
soil. Strands of drooling saliva hung from
the corners of his gaping mouth and at each
corner, there was a curved ivory-coloured
tusk. If Gilbert's nose had been longer and
his ears bigger, he could easily have been
mistaken for an African elephant.

"There you are!" exclaimed Abigail, before turning to me and adding, with a smile, "And this is Gilbert."

"Hello, Gilbert," I said, bending down to make his acquaintance. I extended my open hand and Gilbert came close to investigate. Then he suddenly let out a huge growling grunt followed by a loud, high-pitched squeal. I don't understand pig language, but I don't think he was pleased to see me. This stranger had driven into his haven. His hands smelt of strange chemicals (vets often do) and the stranger hadn't even brought him anything to eat.

"Give him a biscuit, Julian," Abigail said quickly. "That's the best way to make friends with my Gilbert. He's such a sweetie, but he's so greedy!"

I took the packet of digestives from Abigail and fed them one at a time to the fat pig.

Biscuit by biscuit, our relationship moved towards a safe and friendly footing. When Gilbert realized the packet was empty, he lost interest and snuffled away, his curly tail whirling like a helicopter. I'd tackled my first challenge of the morning: making friends with the pig. Next, it was time for my veterinary challenge: sorting out Howard's foot.

Up close, Howard was even bigger than I'd imagined. His withers – the bit where a horse's neck reaches its shoulders – were higher than the top of my head. At least he was good-natured and had no malice. I stroked his strong neck, feeling his power.

"It's this foot," Abigail said, pointing to his left front leg. "He's been lame on and off for a few weeks and we haven't been able to get to the bottom of it. He's seen the farrier who looks after his hooves, but it's not very easy to lift his foot to have a look."

"I'm not surprised," I murmured to myself, expecting this to be difficult but trying to rise to the challenge. I felt down the leg, checking for heat, swelling or pain, and rested my palms on the wall of his dinner-plate-sized hoof. Next, I searched for the pulses in the blood vessels on each side of the fetlock, which is the joint at the back of a horse's foot. One was throbbing more than the other, which led me to suspect an infection under the sole.

"I think there's some infection in the foot, Abigail," I explained. "I'll need to lift his foot, then shave some sole away to drain it out."

It sounded simple but I knew this would be difficult. Howard, gentle as he was, didn't like his feet being picked up, particularly the sore ones. He stubbornly stood with all four feet planted firmly on the ground as I tried to persuade him to let me look.

After what seemed like an hour, I'd made little progress, other than having a sore back and being covered in sweat, which dripped off my nose each time I bent over to pull at the fetlock and lift the limb.

"I should give him some sedative," I suggested. I hoped this might make him less determined to resist, although there was a risk it might make my task harder. A sedated horse, like a sleepy person, might find it harder to balance with one leg up.

I drew up the medication into a syringe and injected it easily into the vein in Howard's neck. Within moments he was calm and sleepy – my sedation seemed to have worked a treat. I had another go at lifting the painful foot and this time he didn't seem to mind.

I arranged my two hoof knives – one big and one small – in the grass alongside

a bucket of water and a brush that Abigail
had prepared, then I set to work with the
larger knife, shaving thin slices of sole off
the bottom of Howard's foot, probing for
the sore area. Even with the patient being
more cooperative, progress was
painstakingly slow.
The hardness of the
pasture and the dry
weather had caused
the soles of his feet
to have solidified
like concrete
and I could only
remove tiny
pieces of the
hoof at a time.
Trimming
the hoof
isn't painful,

because the hoof is like a fingernail or toenail, so it's possible to trim it away without any sensation, just like cutting your nails.

Before long, though, I'd discovered the sore bit – a softer area that made Howard throw his head up and neigh when it was prodded.

"I've found the place," I said to Abigail, who was capably holding on to the lead rope and offering reassurance to Howard. "The infection is in there. If I can just take a few more slices off, I should be able to drain out the pus. I'll use the brush and water to clean the foot a little bit more."

I cleaned the foot to get a better view and planned my attack – which hoof knife would be best to continue with and what angle to cut at?

It was at this point that Gilbert reappeared. He must have heard the noise from Howard and decided to investigate, waddling towards us. First, he put his head in the bucket of water. He thrust his snout to the bottom, making a splash. I think he wanted to rinse the soil and biscuit crumbs away. The splash seemed to startle him, and he gave a sudden jerk of his head, causing the handle of the bucket to swing back over his lop ears. The bucket was stuck. Gilbert panicked. His squeals echoed around inside the bucket and what was left of the water splashed all over his face. A panicking pig, squealing and charging around with a rattling bucket on his head, was too much for Howard. He stomped his foot down, throwing me to the ground in a heap.

The drama was over as quickly as it had started. Gilbert managed to fling the bucket off his head and Howard went back to his sedated snooze, which left me laughing on the grass among the buttercups with Abigail relieved that no serious injury had occurred.

"Oh, naughty Gilbert! You must behave!

I'll put you inside if you're going to interfere!" she shouted at the pig. But Gilbert was oblivious to the drama he had created and headed over to investigate my car. Emmy had woken up after hearing the commotion and was now watching everything from the car window. She wasn't at all sure about the pig. I pulled myself back to my feet, brushing grass seeds and dust out of my hair.

"Let's try that again!" I gasped.

Back in the action and without a pesky pig to intervene, I made better progress. The pocket of infection under Howard's sole was within reach. Now was the time to swap my big knife for the one with the small end – it was perfect for exploring a small but deep crevice. I fumbled around in the grass where I'd left it alongside the bucket and brush.

"Abigail, can you see my other hoof knife?"
I asked. "I left it next to the bucket."

It was nowhere to be seen. Just then,
Emmy barked and I looked across to the car
from where she'd been watching the
events unfold.

"What's up, Em?" I said, puffing with the
ongoing strain of holding up Howard's huge
hoof. It was most unlike her to bark when I
was at work. Then it became clear. Gilbert
swaggered from behind my car – and in his
jaws was my all-important knife!

"Gilbert! You are a naughty pig!"
exclaimed Abigail again. "Come back here
immediately!" Gilbert did not obey, but it
didn't matter. Using the small knife, I made a
final slice and, with a small hissing sound, the
pus that had been causing all the problems
trickled out. Howard's pain immediately
subsided. And so did mine, as I could finally

let go of his heavy foot. I stood up and stretched out my aching back, happy with a successful outcome. Howard, though still sleepy from his sedation, looked much more comfortable.

"Well, I think we deserve a drink," Abigail said. She opened her bag and produced three cans of fizzy orange. "One for you, Julian – you must be thirsty. One for me and, of course, one for Gilbert."

As soon as the cans were opened, Gilbert came running over. I drank mine in one go, then watched as Abigail poured fizzy orange into the gaping mouth of Gilbert. A packet of biscuits and a can of pop – he'd had a good morning.

After we'd finished the drinks, I gave Abigail instructions to bathe Howard's sore foot twice a day, using warm, salty water. I arranged to come back the following week to check it was healing. Abigail thanked me and promised to search the field for the hoof knife that Gilbert had stolen.

"Well, that was eventful, Em," I said as I waved goodbye to the three. "I wonder if next week's visit will be just as entertaining."

As planned, a week later, Emmy and I returned to Abigail's field to see how Howard was getting on. It was another hot day and the afternoon sun was beating down even more. I hoped I wouldn't need to hoist the heavy dray horse's foot for long. The last visit had nearly finished me off!

Emmy soon realized where we were heading. The little dog often had an uncanny knowledge of the lanes and tracks of the Yorkshire Dales with its familiar views of fields, trees, drystone walls and moors. The combination of changes in speed and direction in the car always gave her a clue about where we were. She jumped up and started scanning the field for signs of a renegade pig as we approached. On our way across the bumpy field, I paused to watch the huge form of Howard. He ambled towards the stable block without a trace of a head nod. Any four-legged animal with a lame front leg will walk with a nod as it tries to keep its weight off the painful limb. Even from a distance, I was happy that there had been a big improvement.

At the stables, Abigail and Gilbert were nowhere to be seen. I left Emmy in the car, looking out of the window. In any case, she had seen the commotion last week – the heavy horse with its sore foot and the naughty pig with saliva drooling from his tusks and a tendency for trouble. Emmy had no intention of putting herself in harm's way.

"Hello, Howard," I said to the horse as I

slowly felt down his leg. The throbbing pulse that was there a week ago had eased up. He was much better. Just then, Abigail appeared.

"Hello, Julian," she said, a smile spreading over her face. "As you can see, Howard is doing very well. He's pretty much back to his old self. Gilbert and I have been bathing his foot as you said. Talking of Gilbert and bathing, come and see your favourite pig."

I followed Abigail around to the back of the stable and she put her finger to her lips to gesture for me to be quiet. There, in front of me, was another sight I hadn't seen before, nor expected to see, even on a hot summer's day. Abigail had filled a paddling pool with water. And in the paddling pool, with his head on the side, relaxing in the sun, was Gilbert.

I chuckled. "He looks very happy there."

"Gilbert loves his paddling pool. Especially when it's hot," Abigail explained. "And he feels very bad for stealing your equipment and causing the drama with the bucket last week. So he thought he'd like to say sorry with a small gift. He's got you an ice cream. He's got three ice creams – one for you, one for me and one for himself."

"That's very kind of him, Abigail," I said, laughing, as Abigail called to the pig, "Gilbert, it's ice cream time!"

Difficulty Down on the Dairy Farm

I had to look twice at the message that pinged on my phone.

Lame heifer – visit, please. Urgent.

This was an unusual call-out for a summer evening. For a busy vet – and for that matter, a busy farmer – this was the time to put your feet up after a hard day and recharge your batteries before another action-packed session the next morning. Evening calls are generally the realm of emergencies only – such as a cow or sheep struggling to give birth, a dog that's accidentally eaten something poisonous, or a horse with colic (stomach pain). I couldn't recall ever having been called to an emergency when a cow was lame. Usually, it would wait until morning. Why was this evening's call-out so urgent?

I knew the farmer, Wilf, very well and had visited his dairy herd regularly over the years. Wilf was a cheerful farmer. He had a round red face and was always smiling. His eyes twinkled mischievously, and he laughed and joked constantly, even in times of trouble in the face of adversity. The milk produced by his small herd of cows was bottled on the farm and delivered to everyone in the nearby villages. Wilf's happy face and cheerful whistling, accompanied by the clinking of glass bottles, were a familiar sight and sound to all the locals. He worked hard and I never understood how he wasn't exhausted. Farming cows was a full-time job in itself but acting as a milkman too made his work doubly hard.

I went to Wilf's farm most weeks to carry out simple jobs of all types. He'd always tell a joke or share an amusing story with a cheeky grin. I loved visits to see him, his herd and his old-fashioned farm.

"You said she wouldn't mend and I said she would mend. And I was right," was Wilf's standard line, and then he'd shake with laughter. It seemed that he took great pleasure in his positive approach to problems triumphing over my sometimes-pessimistic outlook. He had total faith in my ability to fix any problem, even though sometimes I didn't share his optimism!

On this cloudless summer evening, as I pulled off the main road on the way to Wilf's farm, I wondered whether I could fix this peculiar case. I expected to see Wilf's cheery face waiting for me, ready with a joke, but when I arrived at the farmyard, he was nowhere to be seen. There was just a small collection of hens scratching around, looking for worms or leftover cow food, their shadows cast long by the setting sun. It was unusually quiet. I climbed out of the car and collected my equipment. I gathered up the usual bottles of medicine and my thermometer and stethoscope. Then I grabbed some extras – my hoof knives, sprays, a halter and ropes – in case I needed to hoist up a sore foot. I also took an extra handful of gloves, just in case things got dirty.

Once I was kitted up, I set about searching for Wilf in the dairy yard, where he gathered the cows before they were milked. His dairy cows, even when enjoying the summer grazing, were never far from the milking parlour – and neither was Wilf. But not today. I continued through the yard, past wooden hay mangers where various cats were sleeping. No doubt they were full of a milky supper and snoozing before a night-time of chasing mice! One fluffy ginger kitten followed me, with its stumpy tail sticking straight up like a flagpole. It meowed with a high-pitched squeak.

"I haven't got anything for you, little one," I said, bending down to stroke its head. The kitten jumped back, hissing.

It was feral, but curious and not sure how to interact with this newcomer to the farm.

I peered into one cowshed after another, the little ginger kitten following me everywhere. There was no sign of Wilf and no lame cow. This was odd. I'd never been to this farm and not found the farmer in the thick of the action. I was certain he wouldn't be resting in the farmhouse kitchen with his feet up. I leant on a gate that overlooked a pasture sloping gently down to the river, which was out of sight in a dip in the distance. The pale green tops of the willow trees that marked the river's course were just visible. I surveyed the tranquil scene. The grass was emerald green and the sky was still deep blue. Swallows swooped, gulping insects in mid-flight. The church clock chimed nine times. It was peaceful and pleasant, and not a bad place to linger, especially with this little

kitten for company. He desperately wanted
to be my friend, I felt sure. If only he could
muster up confidence! I crouched down again
to try and gain his trust. He hissed but didn't
back away this time.

As beautiful as the evening was, and
as smitten with the kitten I'd become,
I was getting anxious about the urgent
predicament that I knew Wilf's cow must be
in. Finally, at the far end of the field, I spotted
the farmer waving his arms behind a slow-
moving, black and white Friesian youngster.
Her head nodded vigorously with each
plodding step and her left front leg hung,
floppy and lifeless, with just the very tip of
her toe touching the grassy ground. Each
time the foot of the painful leg touched the
ground, she threw her head upwards, trying
to relieve the discomfort that was visible
from across the field.

"This must be my patient," I said to myself and the kitten, jumping over the gate into the field to go and help.

"Good evening, Wilf," I said as soon as I was within earshot. "What's going on?"

"Oh, hello!" he said, slightly out of breath. "I've just been fetching her from the far end of this field. She can't walk. Well, she can but not very well. She's just on three legs, I'm afraid.

I just found her this evening down by the river. She's in a lot of pain, so I thought I'd better get you out. I hope you weren't having your tea!" He laughed loudly as usual.

"It's fine, Wilf," I replied quickly. "She looks in a bad way. Do you suppose she can make it to the buildings? I think we'll need to hoist up her leg to see what's going on."

"I'm aiming for that one," he explained, pointing to a small stone building on one side of the field. "I've not used it for cattle for some years. It's too small really, but it's nearer and I think we can make it work."

Progress to the stone building was extremely slow. Even the little kitten, who had decided to come with us, kept stopping and looking around to see why the two humans and one cow were taking so long. As we ambled along, I tried to get a look at the leg and foot to get some idea of what may have happened. The lower limb, from the knee down to the hoof, was hugely swollen and looked like a marrow. It was about three times as big as it should have been. And the smell! It was almost impossible to describe, but stinking, rotting flesh only goes part way to giving an idea!

"What do you think she has done, Wilf?" I asked.

"I don't know," he said. "She's been in this paddock with the rest of the young stock since spring. It stretches down to the river over there – that's where I found her – so there's plenty of fresh water for them all. And the grass is good. There are a few ditches and banks, so she could've fallen. Or one of the others might have kicked her, but they've been together since they were calves, so I'd be surprised if there was any fighting. The rest of them have gone over there." He waved his arm into the distance, in the direction of an adjacent field. "I guess they walked off and she couldn't keep up so decided to stay where she was. She had her foot in the water. It must have been more comfortable that way."

It was a sorry sight. Not only was the leg painful, swollen and infected, but the poor heifer hadn't been able to keep up with the herd when it moved on to the next field. She was left, abandoned, dangling the limp limb into the cold water of the river in an attempt to ease some of the swelling.

"Well, let's hope I can help," was all I could think of to say. My mind was buzzing with ideas of what the problem might be and what I could do about it. "First thing is to get her in there, fasten her up, then I'll try and lift her foot to examine it properly."

"Do you think she'll mend?" Wilf asked,

with his typical smiling optimism. I could tell he thought she would.

"I don't know," I said honestly. It depends on what the problem is. Inwardly, I didn't share the farmer's hopefulness.

The church clock had chimed again by the time Wilf, the heifer, the kitten and I arrived at the small stone building. It must have taken us half an hour to cover just a few hundred metres. There was a dusty floor with some stones protruding from the uneven surface. The heifer looked pleased to be able to rest, but our work was just beginning. Wilf and I looped the rope halter around her nose and ears, and then Wilf secured the halter to a ring set into the wall. The heifer didn't object much. I think she realized we were trying to help.

I looked up and was thankful to see a thick wooden beam stretching across the roof.

I could use this to help lift the limb. With difficulty, I fastened a loop of my rope around the heifer's lower leg. I planned to throw the other end up and over the beam. In this way, I could pull on the rope to raise the foot off the ground, which would allow me to examine it. If there was a stone – or worse, a nail – stuck in the sensitive part of the hoof, I'd need to slice away at the sole with my hoof knife to find and then relieve the problem.

It was easier said than done. First, I had to get the rope over the beam, which was more than a metre above my head. I missed on the first two attempts but on the third try – success! I pulled on the free end, hoping the foot would rise into the air. Nothing happened. So I pulled again, like a bell ringer at the local church. But no luck. The leg was simply too painful for the heifer to lift it.

"Give us a hand, Wilf," I said. "This is gonna need two people!"

Wilf and I hung on to the rope together. Eventually, our combined weight and strength were too much for the heifer and the swollen leg came off the ground and into the air. I looped the free end of the rope around her foot and fastened it to a nearby post. At last, it was secure and I could get on with investigating. The lower leg was infected, soft and red, it smelt so bad that it made my eyes water! I examined the sole and the swollen space between the hooves. Could this be a bad case of dermatitis? If so, I'd never seen one as nasty. I pulled the latex gloves from my pocket and put them on with a twang. I hoped they would protect my fingers from absorbing the awful smell.

I probed and prodded the sole, but I was still no closer to finding the problem.

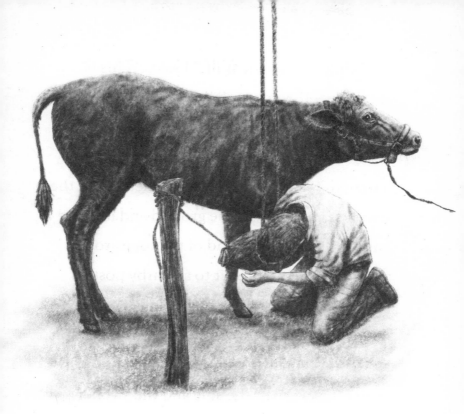

The sole and hoof, though swollen and
smelly, didn't look diseased and there was
no stone or anything spiky lurking in any of
the cracks or crevices. Then, as I felt further
up the leg, the heifer winced and the cause
became obvious.

"Wilf, look!" I exclaimed. "She's got
some sort of ring stuck around her fetlock."

"Well, I never! How on Earth has that got there?" said Wilf. His usual smiling features were replaced by a furrowed brow.

But now was not the time to ask questions. They could come later. The hard rubber ring was about the same size as the hoof. It was cutting off the circulation to the foot and causing awful pain. Now my priority was to get the thing off if I could. After that, I'd have to assess whether the damage was repairable.

I reached for some scissors and edged their ends under the tight band. Snipping at the rubber wasn't working. The material had become solid and unyielding. I'd need to use a surgical scalpel. I hoped I could nick the rubber and release the band without causing damage to the heifer's leg. I poised myself, hoping against hope that she wouldn't move at the wrong moment. If she did, the consequences would be disastrous!

I took a deep breath to calm my nerves and my shaking hands, then aimed the sword-sharp blade at the ring. Success! The blade sliced through the stiff rubber with ease and it pinged off, releasing its tension with another satisfying twang!

"She'll feel better for that!" Wilf chortled, laughing again. His good humour returned.

I prodded the ring. It looked like the rubber tyre from a child's pushchair. "How did that get there?" I asked.

Wilf scratched his head. "Well, we get things washed up by the river after it floods. If she stood on it when it was muddy, and pushed the middle bit of the wheel out, then the tyre could've pinged up around her leg. Poor old girl," he said, gently patting his heifer's neck for comfort. "Just like children, you've got to keep an eye on your animals all the time!"

I reached into my bag for some syringes to draw up doses of painkillers and antibiotics to treat the obvious infection. As I pressed the plunger on each syringe to inject the contents into her rump, I could sense her relief. It had been a most unusual and very unfortunate accident for this youngster, and I was as relieved as she was to have hopefully fixed the problem. Nagging at the back of my mind, though, was another question – would the damage to her tendons and tissues be too bad for her to recover? Only time would tell.

Wilf, on the other hand, was characteristically optimistic.

"You've done a grand job there, Julian. I think you've mended her!"

"Well, I'll come back in a couple of weeks to check on her all the same," I replied.

We left the heifer quietly standing in the small barn as the sun was dipping below the horizon and headed for home. Wilf would return later to check on her with a bucket of water and hay. But for now, my job was done and it was time for me to wash up. As we walked back to the farm, little Ginger, the kitten with the stumpy tail, followed behind us.

Two weeks later, I called back at Wilf's. Passing by his farm on another sunny day, I had some time to spare.

"How's that heifer, Wilf?" I shouted from the window of my car as I drove into his yard.

"Come and look," he chuckled. "She's out here, with her mates."

We walked back to the gate from where I had surveyed his fields in search of the patient that evening. A herd of about fifteen black and white heifers grazed with typical contentment.

"Which one is she?" I asked. "I can't see one that's lame."

"Exactly!" laughed Wilf. "You can't tell. She's completely mended. Just like I said she'd be!" By now, Wilf was holding his sides with laughter. For once, I couldn't help but join in.

A Bad-Tempered Cat and a Grateful Llama

Even without looking out of the window to see the shades of green slowly shifting to orange, or feeling the chill on my cheeks as I trekked over the moors to treat my patients, there was one thing that signified the end of summer and confirmed that autumn was on its way. It was the appearance of a curved wicker cat basket, covered with a silk headscarf, in the waiting room. It was placed carefully on the floor beside the chair occupied by the elegant and well-dressed Lady Roxburgh. And inside the basket was a bad-tempered tortoiseshell cat called Ethel.

Lady Roxburgh spent her summers in North Yorkshire and travelled to London for the winter, taking Ethel along with her on the train each time she made the journey. The final job before heading to the station was a trip to see the vet. Lady Roxburgh always liked to see me, which was hard to understand because her beloved cat really didn't like to see me.

The hissing and spitting began as soon as I lifted Ethel's basket onto the table. As she glared out through the metal grille on the front, I sensed her tension rising. And she could sense mine too.

"Hello again, Ethel," I said, hoping she would be more cooperative today.

But, with lightning speed, Ethel swiped

her claws towards my hand as I tried to unfasten the buckles on the stiff old leather straps that kept the basket door shut. I recoiled quickly. Vets need fast reactions if they are to remain safe. Sharp, well-aimed cats' claws are as painful and dangerous as the hind feet of any thoroughbred horse. I'd learnt this very early in my veterinary career.

"And are you in a good mood today?" I wondered out loud.

Lady Roxburgh explained that Ethel was slightly upset at having been scooped from her bed and bundled into her basket. She knew it meant a trip to the vet followed by a train journey, neither of which she enjoyed.

"But she just needs a check-up, a nail clip and a booster injection," she said. "Oh, and a worming tablet if you've time." It sounded simple, but I knew all these things would be easier said than done.

Most cats don't like their feet being touched, let alone their nails being trimmed. A check-up can be challenging, too, and injections were not Ethel's favourite. But of all the things on Lady Roxburgh's list, it was giving the tablet that I dreaded the most. Of course, the simplest way to give a tablet to a cat is hidden in some tasty food, but cats are experts at finding the hidden pill in even the smelliest tuna or stinkiest cheese. Sometimes there is nothing for it but to open the cat's mouth and try to pop the tablet in, pushing it far enough back that it is swallowed rather than spat out again. Giving a tablet in this way brings the vet's fingers into another danger zone – the needle-sharp teeth. A cat bite is a very nasty thing and can often lead to an infection.

Once again, Ethel hissed and spat as Lady Roxburgh removed her from the safety of her basket. My mind raced as I calculated which of the challenges I should tackle first.

I decided on my plan of attack:

1) Check-up
2) Vaccination
3) Nail clip
4) Worm tablet

Dealing with the simplest first would allow Ethel to relax. I'd leave the most dangerous job to last. If it proved impossible, then at least I'd have done the other three tasks and Lady Roxburgh could take the tablet with her and hide it in Ethel's first meal in London.

I edged my way to the table and cautiously stroked her fluffy head, glancing into her ears and feeling her neck to check for lumps or bumps. So far, so good. I slipped my stethoscope along Ethel's ribs to listen to her heart. It was going quickly but sounded strong. All the time, there was a low grumbling from her throat, like a wild animal waiting to defend itself by launching an attack! Suddenly, she let out a louder hissing noise and swiped her paw at my hand again, narrowly missing my exposed arm. It was at that moment that I realized my examination was over. Any cat who could react that quickly must be one hundred per cent healthy, I decided. The needle slid into the skin of the scruff of her neck with only a hint of a complaint – this time a low growling, like a dog that didn't want to give up with a bone.

"Well, Ethel looks in excellent health, Lady Roxburgh," I declared confidently. "And I've administered her vaccination."

I reached for a pair of tough leather gauntlets for the nail clipping. I could only wear one glove because it was impossible to operate the clippers through the thick material, but at least one hand would be

protected. Some lunges, jabs and prods from
Ethel, like a sparring boxer, left only two
scratches on my exposed hand. I breathed
half a sigh of relief. Three out of four jobs
were ticked off, but I still had the tablet to
give. This was the part I was dreading most.
I unwrapped it from its foil packet with
sweaty hands, steeling myself for a vicious

attack from the increasingly annoyed cat. Just then, there was a loud knock on the consulting room door.

"Julian, there's a bit of an emergency," said Sylvia, one of the receptionists. "There's a llama at the top of the dale at High Leys. It sounds like there's been a bad accident. They think its jaw is broken and he's in a lot of pain. Can you go immediately? It's at the 'high buildings'. Do you know where that is?"

I looked at Lady Roxburgh, who had already started talking. "Oh, Julian. Don't worry about the tablet. I can give it to her this evening. I'm sure she'll take it. She's always ravenously hungry after a day's travelling so I can hide it in some food."

As I released Ethel from my gauntlet grip, she gave me one final glare and hissed indignantly before sauntering back to her owner for a welcomed stroke behind the ear.

Lady Roxburgh fussed her fondly and Ethel soon let out a soothing purr. I chuckled to myself, thinking about my patients and their owners. Whilst I knew both appreciated my care, I also knew that I wasn't a favourite with all of my patients.

I'd had a lucky escape with Ethel and my fingers would stay safe, at least for now. But a llama with a broken jaw – he wasn't so fortunate. Surely this would be an even bigger challenge.

I wished Lady Roxburgh and Ethel well for their winter in London, hoping they would have a pleasant train journey and success with the worming tablet. Then I grabbed the equipment I thought I might need for this unusual crisis, called Emmy and hastily headed for the door.

The llama farm was one of the furthest away from the practice, situated right at the top of the dale and on the edge of a bleak and wind-swept moor. The "high buildings" were at the very furthest part of the farm and used as a temporary shelter for grazing animals that needed attention. There are lots of high barns like this over the hills, where poorly cattle or sheep would have been collected, rather than bringing them back down to the farm. However, I don't expect many llamas have been examined in such an old and traditional building. Llamas aren't the usual North Yorkshire farm creature, but they've become popular in recent years. And, just like Mr Hawthorne and his alpacas, more farmers in the Dales were keeping unusual breeds, which keeps the job of a country vet interesting! I first became interested in llamas soon after starting work as a vet and they're fascinating to treat. When annoyed, llamas can be just as bad-tempered as Ethel the cat and won't think twice before spitting a glob of smelly mucus, saliva and partly chewed grass directly into a human's face as well as at each other. It's pretty disgusting! Angry llamas will also fight each other – biting or kicking with great accuracy. *Was this the reason for today's problem?* I wondered.

"This is a strange one, Em," I mused. "As if treating a llama isn't odd enough, this one has a problem with its mouth. The farmer thinks it might have a broken jaw." Emmy just cocked her head and pricked her ears. I always imagined she could understand exactly what I was saying

and that she would reply by saying something like, "Oh dear. That sounds nasty. Will you be able to repair it with some wire, as you do with a cat that's been hit by a car?" That would have been a good question. I'd never seen a llama with a broken jaw before, so I wasn't exactly sure what I'd be able to do.

The winding roads got narrower the further I travelled, demanding care and concentration. As we headed up the dale, the views became more spectacular. The moors were always beautiful, but at this time of year, the colours were starting to change. The purple tops of heather had faded to a dusty brown, while the lower slopes of the valley were peppered with trees of all shades. Some were still green, but most were rusty or golden. The occasional rowan tree added sparks of colour, with bright red or orange berries glowing in the pale sun as it descended towards the horizon.

I turned off the main road and up the long farm track to the highest buildings at High Leys Farm. Emmy started squeaking with excitement, anticipating an autumn walk. She was imagining leaping over the tufty bushes, scurrying between the sparse rowan trees and diving around the gritstone rocks that littered the hillsides around these parts. She knew them well. But that would have to wait.

"Not yet, Em. Maybe later if there's time," I said, ruffling her ears. I had a big job ahead of me and I didn't know if I would be successful.

Suzanne, the farmer, was waiting for me outside the solid stone buildings. They were as isolated as their name suggested but strong and sturdy. I'm sure they'd been there for a hundred years, yet there were no signs of wear or tear, despite the fearsome winter weather that always gripped these places for months on end. The worried farmer wasted no time explaining the situation.

"It's my young boy, Rowan. I don't know what's happened, but his jaw is lopsided and he's in a lot of pain. He was fine this morning, but something happened to him during the afternoon," Suzanne explained. I smiled at the llama's name. I'd just been thinking about rowan trees and their berries, so it was a funny coincidence, and I took it as a good sign.

I climbed out of the car, leaving Emmy to dream of her walk. There was a distinct chill in the air as it was already late in the day and the sun had lost much of its earlier warmth.

"He's inside," said Suzanne, pushing open a wooden door. "I've tried to make him as comfortable as possible, but I've been worrying myself sick about him all afternoon. I know we're not supposed to have favourites, but Rowan is such a wonderful boy."

Rowan was safely secured in a large, straw-filled pen. He looked forlorn, with a thin strand of blood-tinged saliva dangling from his floppy mouth. He was wearing a head collar, just like a pony. Suzanne wasted no time in taking hold of the collar and steadying the distressed Rowan, and I followed into the pen.

"Don't worry, lad," I said. "We're here to help." Llamas (and their alpaca cousins) don't like their heads or faces to be touched. I hoped my words would offer some comfort. Once I managed to calm Rowan enough to open his mouth, it was clear there was a big problem. The front part of his lower jaw was loose. A couple of teeth were missing and there was an obvious break on the outside of the front teeth. "Oh, dear. His jaw is broken, just as you thought," I told Suzanne, explaining my findings to her.

"Oh no, poor boy! I wonder if he could've been kicked?" she said. "The boys sometimes become bad-tempered and start fighting. They can kick with some power and accuracy, though I've never known one to get kicked in the face!"

We didn't know what might have caused the injury, but it didn't matter. What did matter was whether it would be possible to fix it. Suzanne echoed the concerns that were running through my head. "Will you have to put him down?" she asked, fearing the worst.

For a few moments, I didn't know what to say so I said nothing. I carefully wiggled the broken jaw, probing carefully and cautiously, trying to work out which bits were solid and which bits were loose, and if there was a way of stabilizing the fracture. I've fixed the broken jaws of many cats and the occasional dog – victims of car accidents, leaping over too-high walls, or running races that result in crashing into a tree or gate at speed. So far in my veterinary career, I'd never had to repair a fractured llama jaw. Luckily, vets are trained to think and act on our feet, making quick decisions and judgements based on experience and knowledge, but also to transfer that knowledge to treat any type of animal. After a swift assessment, I believed I could fix this llama's fracture using the same method I would use for a cat or a dog.

I explained my plan to Suzanne. "I think I can thread some orthopaedic wire around his teeth, If it aligns and I can get it stable, there's a good chance his broken jaw will heal."

Suzanne almost burst into tears of happiness, relieved there was a chance to save her favourite young llama. It often seems to happen that farmers' favourite animals are the ones who succumb to the most horrible illness and accidents. Rowan was a llama with lots of personality and was very popular on the farm. Suzanne couldn't imagine what it would be like without him.

I went back to my car to rummage for the equipment I'd need. By a good chance, orthopaedic wire and some wire twisters were in the handful of kit I'd hastily grabbed before I left the practice. Emmy lifted her head from her usual position on my car seat as if to say, "Are we going for that walk now?" But she quickly went back to sleep when she realized this was far from the case. I needed more things, too. Local anaesthetic, syringes, needles, painkillers. And a whole lot of luck!

Back with Rowan, I quickly injected him with some painkillers to reduce some of the soreness. It seemed likely he had been kicked by another herd mate, which was painful

enough, but a broken jaw would be even worse.
Next, I drew up some local anaesthetic into a
syringe. This is the stuff that dentists use to
numb small areas for fillings or to take out a
tooth. I carefully inserted the needle under
Rowan's gum line and injected small amounts
to provide some extra pain relief. At first, when
the needle went in, he recoiled – I think it stung
a bit. But soon, his lower jaw was comfortably
numb. So far, all was going to plan. The next
bit – when I tried to place the wire inside the
jaw – was critical. I opened the packet and
cut off a length. I planned to thread the wire
around teeth on either side of the fracture line,
then form a loop and twist the ends to tighten
the wire, pulling the broken jaw together and
stabilizing the break. I hoped it would work and
that Rowan would behave and cooperate.
I didn't want him spitting directly into my face –
I was right in his firing line!

The first end of the wire went in fairly easily, between two teeth. It looked and felt secure. Next, I had to thread it between two other teeth. This proved to be more difficult. The teeth in this part of the mouth had been damaged by the kick, so the wire didn't hold. Each time I tried to tighten the loop, the wire pulled off, leaving the jaw still loose and me filled with increasing despair. Suzanne wasn't looking at this point, too worried to watch but constantly offering quiet words of reassurance to calm Rowan.

Finally, I managed to secure the wire. I pulled on each end to tighten the loop, twisting the ends together, the way a wrapper secures a toffee. Each twist turned the loop more tightly. Rowan's jaw was slowly being pulled into alignment. I smiled to myself, just as the llama's smile was re-forming.

"It's working!" I said triumphantly.

"Just a couple more twists and the jaw will be all lined up." I stood back to admire my work. Rowan's repaired mouth was firm and stable. With luck, he'd make a full recovery.

"That looks almost back to normal!" exclaimed Suzanne, delighted at what I'd managed to achieve.

"I hope this will work," I added cautiously. "If all goes well, I should come back in a few weeks, once it's healed, to take the wire out. Shall we see if he can eat?"

Suzanne let go of his head collar. There was a heap of hay in the corner of the barn. To our delight, Rowan wandered straight over, grabbed a mouthful and started chewing with vigorous intent, as if nothing had happened. My plan had worked. Back at the car, I couldn't wait to tell Emmy all about it.

"Well, Em, it worked like a dream. I fixed Rowan just like I would have fixed a cat!"

I said, cheerily, pulling out of the long farm drive and onto the narrow road back down the dale. There was just enough light left to illuminate the sky to the west. "I think there is still time for a walk."

As we reached the top of the valley, Emmy wagged her tale with excitement as I pulled the car to a stop. I zipped up my gilet and pulled my collar around my neck as a gentle brisk breeze blew across the Dales, marking the end of warm summer evenings. After a short walk, I stopped at a familiar viewpoint, sitting on the stone wall and watching the sun fade behind the clouds. In this distance, I heard the horn of a train and I thought fondly of Ethel and Lady Roxburgh on their own journey home.

ABOUT THE AUTHOR

JULIAN NORTON is a respected veterinary surgeon, regular on the best-loved series *The Yorkshire Vet* and author of many novels for adults, including *Horses, Heifers and Hairy Pigs: The Life of a Yorkshire Vet* and *All Creatures: Heart-Warming Tales from a Yorkshire Vet*. Having worked in Yorkshire at various animal practices, he became a partner in a practice at which Alf Wight (better known under his pseudonym of James Herriot) worked. In 2019, Julian set up Sandbeck Veterinary Centre in Wetherby. He also spends a lot of time working in Thirsk, a town that he has made his home. Julian continues to appear on *The Yorkshire Vet* as well as regularly appearing as a guest on television shows and literary events. *Adventures with a Yorkshire Vet: Lambing Time and Other Animal Tales* is Julian's first collection of animal stories for children.

ABOUT THE AUTHOR

JULIAN NORTON is a respected veterinary surgeon, regular on the best-loved series *The Yorkshire Vet* and author of many novels for adults, including *Horses, Heifers and Hairy Pigs: The Life of a Yorkshire Vet* and *All Creatures: Heart-Warming Tales from a Yorkshire Vet*. Having worked in Yorkshire at various animal practices, he became a partner in a practice at which Alf Wight (better known under his pseudonym of James Herriot) worked. In 2019, Julian set up Sandbeck Veterinary Centre in Wetherby. He also spends a lot of time working in Thirsk, a town that he has made his home. Julian continues to appear on *The Yorkshire Vet* as well as regularly appearing as a guest on television shows and literary events. *Adventures with a Yorkshire Vet: Lambing Time and Other Animal Tales* is Julian's first collection of animal stories for children.

ACKNOWLEDGEMENTS

Writing my second children's book has been another great experience. I've recalled some lovely stories about my favourite patients during spring and summer in Yorkshire. I must thank all the animals and their owners for allowing me to treat them. Without you, this book would not exist!

Thank you to Charlie Wilson, my editor, and art director Louise Jackson at Walker Books. Everyone at MBA books who has helped to make my journey into the literary world easier to navigate. Jo Weaver, my amazing and talented illustrator, has once again brought my words to life. I can't thank you enough!

The talented people at Daisybeck Studios, thank you too! Especially Paul Stead and Laura Blair, whose passion and enthusiasm are almost limitless. I'll always be so grateful for the very special privilege of being able to share the things I love with millions of viewers on the telly through *The Yorkshire Vet*.

Anne, my wife and assistant editor, continues to help with good guidance and wise words. Thank you again.

Finally, my best friend with four legs, Emmy. You feature in this book as a constant presence, something you do in my life in general. Your vigour and lust for life are a constant inspiration.